The Memory Lingers On

The Memory Lingers On

More British Railways working steam

Mike Esau

· RAILWAY HERITAGE ·
from
The NOSTALGIA Collection

First published in 2009

British Library Cataloguing in Publication Data

A catalogue record for this book is available from the British Library.

ISBN 978 1 85794 340 5

Silver Link Publishing Ltd
The Trundle
Ringstead Road
Great Addington
Kettering
Northants NN14 4BW

Tel/Fax: 01536 330588
email: sales@nostalgiacollection.com
Website: www.nostalgiacollection.com

Printed and bound in the Czech Republic

Near Betchworth: 'U' 2-6-0 No 31622
This is not the most perfectly executed picture, but I have included it since it shows my old Royal Enfield bicycle on the right, which I often used for journeys of up to 70 miles a day to photograph steam when I was a teenager. I still have this bike and even now it (and me!) is capable of the occasional short outing for old times' sake. My brother and I – whose bicycle you can also just see – are standing on the path that followed the line towards Reigate from the south side of the level crossing by the station. The driver of No 31622, with a train for Reading, has just shut off steam for the Betchworth stop. Notice the oil lamp between the two route discs over the buffer beam – perhaps the fireman has forgotten to remove it.

Near Brasted Halt: 'H' 0-4-4T No 31324
As I have related in my earlier 'Memories' books, in the early 1960s I used Lambretta scooters to get around the country on my photographic expeditions. My first machine, an Li 125 that I bought new in 1960, is parked near the overbridge as No 31324 propels its train from Dunton Green towards Westerham.

Contents

Half title **Cole: '2P' 4-4-0 No 40700**
Happy memories: it is about teatime on an idyllic warm summer afternoon at this Somerset & Dorset line station in 1959. The '2P' is leaving with a stopping train for Bournemouth West made up of four Maunsell coaches. My two fellow photographers are probably discussing the merits of the pictures they have just taken. Another view of Cole appears on page 49.

Page 2 **Marlow: '14XX' 0-4-2T No 1474**
On 20 January 1962 the weather is very different from Cole, but the wet conditions add to the atmosphere of this picture. What a wonderful ornate gas lamp that is – I wonder if it has survived. My brother is contemplating the neat little tank engine as it prepares to leave with 'The Marlow Donkey' on the short run to Bourne End. Seen in the background is the one-road locomotive shed with its attendant water tower.

Title page **Bournemouth Central**
One of the pleasures on offer at Bournemouth Central was the superb view of the comings and goings at the locomotive shed, which could be enjoyed from the long station platforms. On 3 June 1967, with barely a month to go before the end of steam on the Southern, the main event here is the arrival of 'A4' No 4498 *Sir Nigel Gresley* on an A4 Locomotive Preservation Society rail tour from Waterloo. Memories could be in the making for the five young lads in the foreground – the adult with them is perhaps explaining what the unusually shiny locomotive is. By today's standards the enthusiasts lining the wall by the shed are noticeably lacking in camera gear.

Above **Ballaghaderreen CIE: 'G2' 2-4-0 No 654**
I thought this might be an interesting picture for the beginning of the book. During the course of our honeymoon to the west of Ireland in September 1962, my wife and I visited the steam-worked Ballaghaderreen and Loughrea branches, more pictures of which appear on pages 88 and 89. On 11 September the 11.50am branch train is waiting to leave for Kilfree Junction on the main line to Sligo. Alison is leaning out of the coach and I recall we were the only passengers. The 2nd Class return fare for the two of us was 7s 6d. We vividly remember that the coach smelled of damp and, as we rolled along the lightly laid track to the junction, green water slopped around in the bowl of the large compartment light fitting.

Introduction

I am delighted to be able to present a third selection of my photographs from the British Railways steam era as a follow-up to my last 'Memories' book, *Memories are made of this*, published in 2008. The title of this book is adapted from that of the song composed by Irving Berlin – 'The song is ended but the melody lingers on' – steam is ended but the memory lingers on. The pictures are set out in five sections – 'Main line action', 'Secondary and cross country lines', 'Branch lines', 'Locomotive sheds' and 'Freight workings'. Other 'Memories' were captured in my book *Steam's Last Stand*, also published in 2008, which focussed on the demise of steam in the North West in the ten years or so up to 1968.

Since I wrote the Introduction to *Memories are made of this*, the inexorable rise of digital photography has meant that fewer people still use film, a recent significant event being the demise of the famous 'Kodachrome', much favoured by many railway photographers. For those who have stayed with colour transparency film, it is becoming increasingly difficult to have it processed, perhaps entailing a time-consuming special journey or accepting the risk of sending precious material through the post. On the digital side, quite apart from the mainstream SLRs, there are now some very high-specification compact digital cameras available, ideal to cover things such as special events, works open days, family occasions and so on. The dedicated film scanner is another modern piece of equipment that offers the facility to extract the best from transparencies and negatives, especially in conjunction with the use of 'Photoshop' software. This technology can resurrect what might have been regarded in the pre-digital age as 'write-off' pictures, so never throw old transparencies and negatives away! Nevertheless I have used my darkroom to make the black and white prints for this book and feel that there is nothing to match the satisfaction in producing a really good-quality result by the traditional development process.

Of the colour pictures, one has been 'rescued' – the photograph that appears on page I showing Nos 34006/57 emerging from Chilcompton Tunnel. On this occasion I was attempting to use two cameras at the same time, my Voightlander Bessa II loaded with black and white film and a Zeiss Ikon Super Ikonta containing Ektachrome colour transparency film. At this point in time some 43 years on I can't recall exactly how I was holding the cameras, but the result was that, while both pictures were perfectly exposed, my slightly incorrect alignment of the colour camera had the result that the front of the leading loco was too close to the right-hand side of the transparency. However, thanks to the wonders of 'Photoshop', some more of the image from the right-hand side of the picture has been cloned in, balancing up the composition. Needless to say, the rest of the picture has not been altered in any way, and after all these years how pleased I am to see it as it should have originally been taken!

Looking back to the days of working steam, long before the advent of the mobile phone and the Internet, I have often wondered how we found out what was going on and where. I suppose sometimes it was luck, being in the right place at the right time, but as there was so much steam activity you were unfortunate if you did not come away from the lineside with something worthwhile. Train timetables published by the various BR Regions (and maybe official working timetables if you could gain access to them) were of course essential when out taking pictures. There was also the information contained in the railway press, but lead times were so long that news was often well out of date before you read it. Rail tours, though, were advertised in advance, so there was usually plenty of time to plan photographing them, even if timings were generally not as detailed as are available today. More important, then as now, was local knowledge of workings and a flourishing enthusiast grapevine. This was often fed from official sources, perhaps through people who worked in useful areas on British Railways such as traffic control offices.

Map-reading was an important skill in finding the best locations. The earlier series of 1-inch Ordnance Survey maps are now invaluable, not only as an aid to writing captions, but also because they show many lines that have since been closed and the locations of the stations on them. Of course the weather has been a constant source of interest to railway photographers over the years. Without the benefits of satellite technology, weather forecasts, usually tied in with 'The News' on radio and television, were considerably less reliable and more sketchy compared to what is available today. But as there was so much to see, I can't recall the weather forecast making much difference to planning a day's photography – you just went and took pot luck, which is why I suppose many of my pictures of working steam are taken in indifferent weather. Did it really matter anyway, given the rich diversity of the railway infrastructure, which added so much to the atmosphere of photographs of the time?

Another great difference between now and the 1950s/'60s was the availability of food to sustain you on a long day of photography. Imagine arriving in the evening at somewhere fairly out of the way like Milford Haven in west Wales. Where to eat? Meals in hotels were expensive and usually served at fixed times, often at, say, 7pm for dinner.

Pubs might offer sandwiches during the day ('I'll see what I can do, Sir') but generally only served drink, and garages invariably confined themselves to the sale of petrol and other motoring necessities. The range of restaurants we take for granted today did not exist, so it was often a fish and chip shop that came to the rescue, or one of the welcome Chinese restaurants that invariably seemed to be waiting, even in the remotest of towns.

Today interest in steam railway photography, especially by its younger practitioners, is perhaps as great as it has ever been. The lengths to which photographers will go for perhaps only one or two pictures is impressive, maybe involving a drive of hundreds of miles in a day. The loss of steam age infrastructure means that light and perspective must now be used to the fullest extent possible to maximise the impact of an image.

However, even with perfect conditions photography on today's national railway network can sadly be a frustrating and stressful occupation. It is difficult to find good locations where the lineside is not obscured by trees and bushes, especially in the southern half of the country. At stations, once wonderful locations for pictures, photographers are now sometimes questioned by railway and security staff when trying to innocently exercise their craft. However, the challenges of photographing steam on the main line are happily still with us, enlivened by the arrival of 'A1' No 60163 on the scene, which recalls the thrill of capturing a brand new locomotive on film for the first time. Significant milestones are there to be recorded as well, such as the first steam-hauled through train from London to Swanage on 2 May 2009 hauled by No 34067, which was met by enthusiastic crowds at the end of its journey. Hopefully in the near future the Bluebell Railway will arrive at East Grinstead through a cleared

Imberhorne cutting, which is shown in the 1958 picture below. Who would have believed such things possible in the 'dark ages' for steam at the end of the 1960s and early 1970s?

Several people have kindly helped me with this latest 'Memories' book, especially where my memory has 'malingered' rather than 'lingered', so if there are any errors I must make the excuse of putting it down to the passage of the years! However, I have done all I can to ensure that the captions are accurate, even though I can't produce precise dates for some of the photographs, but I hope their interest will make up for this. Once again I must thank 'the two Johns' (John Edgington and John Gilks), for their invaluable help looking through and commenting on the content of the pictures; Roger Merry-Price, for some wonderful research and detective work; Roger Cruse, for allowing me access to his collection of various railway periodicals for research; my long-time friend Gerry Siviour, for helping me with information for some of the captions, often recalling our trips from long ago; my brother David, for assistance on dates and for reminding me about things I had forgotten about during the journeys we made together; John Beckett and John Stretton, for confirming some of the locations in my pictures; and Peter, Will, Mick and the staff at Silver Link for making this book possible. Finally, my thanks as always to my wife Alison for her help in the arrangement and sequencing of the pictures. She also offered invaluable comments and suggestions on the text, and not least allowed me to use one of her splendid Hayling Island branch colour pictures.

Mike Esau
Richmond, Surrey
2009

Imberhorne cutting: '4MT' 2-6-4T No 80152
This photograph is especially topical some half century on. The Bluebell Railway, in its bid to reach East Grinstead, has made a start on the removal of rubbish that blocks this section of line. Some idea of the depth and width of the cutting can be appreciated in this picture of No 80152 in February 1958, as it heads into the evening sun with a train from East Grinstead to Lewes, composed of a solitary LB&SCR compartment coach.

Main-line action

While photography on main lines was rewarding, it often showed up the limitations of the cameras available at the time. The principal problem was whether you would be able to 'stop' the train, especially if using a slower shutter speed required by the colour films of the day, few of which were rated above 64 ASA. Among my old photographic invoices I have found a couple of Camera Test Certificates issued by Bowens in Gerrard Street, London, W1 '(Established 1923)'. They include a lovely photograph of nearly 30 white-coated camera technicians working away at their benches – 'Now the largest camera repair organisation in Europe', proudly proclaims the Certificate. In April 1968 they tested my Voightlander Bessa II, which revealed that its Synchro-Compur shutter speeds were reasonably accurate up to 1/250th of a second, but the marked 1/500th of a second was only 1/400th, so there could be problems stopping fast-moving trains. Fortunately in steam days main-line speeds were nothing like the 100mph-plus they can be now, which requires the accuracy of a camera fitted with an electronic shutter if you are going to obtain a sharp result. As a matter of interest I bought a pre-war vintage 6cm x 9cm Super Ikonta when I was in Germany in the mid-1950s, but in 1959 was able to upgrade to a Bessa II. I bought this from the Soho Camera Centre in Shaftesbury Avenue, W1, which was run by the genial 'Herbie' J. Beck. I still have the invoice for this camera, for which I paid £27 10s 0d, a fair bit of money 50 years ago. In turn I later part-exchanged it for the same model of camera but with a five-element Color Heliar lens, and, together with other cameras, used it for black and white work to the end of BR steam in 1968. In good condition Bessa IIs are worth several hundred pounds today.

Both in size and age there was a wide range of locomotives to be seen on the main line in the BR steam years, and these were supplemented by the arrival of the Standard classes from 1951 to 1960. I think something of this variety is shown in the photographs that follow. As I mentioned in my previous book, *Memories are made of this*, perhaps the most amazing thing was the use of vintage 4-4-0s in front-line service right up to 1959. A reminder of this is provided by my pictures of Nos 3440 and 31753 on the following page. I made several trips to locations such as Sole Street bank where the game old Maunsell 4-4-0s stormed up the 3 miles or so of 1 in 100 from Rochester on summer weekends hauling trains much heavier than you would think they were capable of dealing with. Displaced by electrification, with no more work to do, several ended up discarded at Feltham (page 102). Sadly also long gone are the holiday trains that ran on a few Saturdays a year, such as the Ramsgate to Wolverhampton train and the '4700' Class 2-8-0 working from Penzance, both shown on page 25. To capture these on film added greatly to the satisfaction of a day's photography.

Langford Bridge: 'A1' 4-6-2 No 60139
Sea Eagle
On this fine afternoon the 'A1' is heading south past Langford Bridge signal box, situated in the valley of the River Ivel south of Biggleswade, with an up express consisting of an interesting range of coaching stock. Who would have thought then that a brand new 'A1' would be once again passing this spot nearly 50 years later in 2009?

Paddington: 'City' 4-4-0 No 3440 *City of Truro*
Victoria: 'L1' 4-4-0 No 31753
Towards the end of the 1950s 4-4-0s could still be seen on main-line duty at London termini as shown in these two pictures. In 1957 No 3440 was restored to working condition and was not only used on Didcot, Newbury & Southampton (DNS) line trains, but amazingly in the summer of 1958 had a fairly regular working from the capital with the 6.20pm semi-fast commuter service to Reading. This train is seen leaving Paddington.

A little later, when the first phase of the Kent Coast electrification was inaugurated, the final main-line steam train to the Kent coast was the 8.52pm train to Dover on 14 June 1959. As it was midsummer there was just about enough light left for me to be able to photograph the old 'L1', adorned with a wreath, leaving the station for the last time with this train. A lone figure on a nearby platform waves farewell.

Euston: 'Britannia' 4-6-2 No 70032 *Tennyson*;
'Princess Coronation' 4-6-2 No 46229 *Duchess of Hamilton*
No 70032 is approaching the station, which is still very much of
the steam age, with no hint of the monumental changes that were
to take place with the arrival of overhead electrification and the
associated rebuilding work.

As a change from the usual view of trains looking along the
arrival platforms, I have photographed No 46229 at Platform 6
facing the buffer stops. This angle gives some sense of the dark,
sooty but very atmospheric nature of parts of the old Euston.

St Pancras: '2P' 4-4-0 No 40548
King's Cross: 'A3' 4-6-2 No 60108 *Gay Crusader*

A short walk down from Euston, Kentish Town shed's rather run-down-looking '2P' is on station pilot duties at St Pancras carrying two lamps, one white and one red, over the buffer beam. This '2P' was withdrawn in January 1961.

At next-door King's Cross more modern motive power is to be seen. No 60108 is beginning its 203-mile journey north with the 'Yorkshire Pullman'. In 1961 the train left London at 5.25pm, first stop Doncaster at 7.50pm, arriving at Harrogate at 9.20pm.

Right **Marylebone: '4MT' 2-6-4T
No 42282, 'L1' 2-6-4T No 67756**
A quiet moment at the station in 1959 –
two railwaymen chat beside the Fairburn
tank, not long arrived with a train from
Aylesbury. In the adjacent platform the
'L1', which would be withdrawn in early
1962, makes an interesting comparison
with the LMS Derby-built locomotive. The
advertisement on the board to the right of
the 'L1' proclaims that 'They come out
best on Kodak film' – I would, however,
have been using Ilford HP3 black and
white film, though I concede there was
nothing to beat Kodachrome for colour!

Below **Paddington: three 'Castle' 4-6-0s, (l-r) unidentified,
No 5070 *Sir Daniel Gooch* and No 7008 *Swansea Castle***
In contrast, at nearby Paddington all is bustle and noise as these
three 'Castles' wait to leave with trains for the West, including the
5.55pm 'The Red Dragon', which ran through to Carmarthen
where it was due to arrive shortly before midnight. Who, I wonder,
is the neatly attired elderly gentleman contemplating the 'Castle'
on 'The Red Dragon'? He slightly resembles that doyen of
locomotive performance and train timing, the legendary Cecil J.
Allen (although I only saw him in photographs), but whoever he
is, he is perhaps anticipating a good run down to Wales!

Victoria: 'C' 0-6-0 No 31317
I am on board a Victoria-bound electric unit in the days when the carriage door windows could be opened. My train has been stopped for signals outside the terminus, which has given me the opportunity to capture this pleasing shot of the 'C' as it works an empty train of Hastings-gauge stock up the 1 in 62 gradient towards Grosvenor Bridge.

London Bridge: 'Schools' 4-4-0 No 30925 *Cheltenham*, 7 October 1962 Carrying a '70D' Basingstoke shed plate, the nicely cleaned 'Schools' is waiting to leave with the Railway Correspondence & Travel Society (RCTS) 'Sussex Coast' rail tour. No 30925 took the train to Brighton and, after a return trip to Seaford behind 'E6' No 32418 and 'Terrier' No 32636, it came back to London Bridge behind 'K' 2-6-0 No 32353. *Cheltenham* was withdrawn shortly afterwards in December 1962, but was preserved and is now part of the National Collection.

Above **Graveney marshes: 'N1' 2-6-0**

On summer Saturdays in the late 1950s there was a constant procession of trains to photograph between London and the Kent Coast resorts, hauled by a wide variety of locomotives such as the Maunsell 'Moguls', more usually seen on freight workings. Taking its turn in the queue of trains heading for Victoria, the 'N1' is blowing off steam impatiently, restarting from a signal check between Whitstable and Faversham.

Right **Robertsbridge: 'U1' 2-6-0 No 31902**

On this lovely summer afternoon in 1957 the 2-6-0 is coasting into Robertsbridge with a train from Charing Cross to Hastings, which includes a Pullman car. To the immediate right of the locomotive is the little signal cabin controlling the Kent & East Sussex line to Rolvenden and Tenterden.

Above **Sturt Lane Farnborough: 'West Country' 4-6-2 No 34038 *Lynton***

No 34038 was withdrawn in June 1966 so was among the last of the class in use, but was allowed to get into a filthy state. Cleaners (or maybe enthusiasts) have made an attempt to scrape some of the oily grime off its casing, but the low angle of the sun on this up train shows up the limitations of their efforts.

Below **Basingstoke: Rebuilt 'West Country' 4-6-2 No 34026 *Yes Tor*, 'Battle of Britain' 4-6-2 No 34057 *Biggin Hill***

The rain-soaked shiny platforms add to the atmosphere of this picture of the two Bulleid 'Pacifics' passing. No 34057 is on a Bournemouth shed duty, while the fireman on No 34026, John Roscoe, sporting characteristic knotted handkerchief headgear, looks ready for what will probably be a fast run up to Waterloo.

Above **Southampton Central: Rebuilt 'Merchant Navy' 4-6-2 No 35016 *Elders Fyffes***
Although modern signalling is very efficient, it cannot compete with the visual appeal of a gantry of semaphores, such as this fine example that has featured in many photographs over the years. Amidst a haze of drifting smoke, No 35016 is coasting into the station with an up express from Bournemouth. Faintly visible to the left of centre are the cranes in the New Docks.

Right **Basingstoke: 'West Country' 4-6-2 No 34015 *Exmouth***
This gantry, which was smaller than the one at the other end of Basingstoke station, controlled westbound departures. The driver of No 34015 has eased his locomotive to allow it to coast through with a non-stop down express. Just departing from the adjacent platform is a train from the Midlands to Bournemouth. Visible beyond the 'West Country', an unidentified Type 4 (later Class 45) diesel waits to work an inter-regional train to the north.

Between Bramley and Basingstoke: 'Hall' 4-6-0 No 5901 *Hazel Hall*
The morning of 10 December 1960 was a cold clear one, ideal to photograph Reading shed's smartly turned-out and memorably named 'Hall'. The locomotive makes a lovely sight as it heads south with a short train of Bulleid coaches bound for Portsmouth & Southsea. My brother has reminded me that later in the day, after the weather had deteriorated, we took refuge at Bramley station where there was a nice fire in the down-side waiting room, which helped us to get warm after standing by the lineside.

Between Bramley and Mortimer: 'Lord Nelson' 4-6-0 No 30864
Sir Martin Frobisher,* 'West Country' 4-6-2 No 34105 *Swanage
We took more photographs along the line on 10 December, including this 'Lord Nelson', which is heading north with an inter-regional train, probably the Bournemouth to York service. The line between Basingstoke and Reading was a busy one for steam passenger workings between the South Coast, the Midlands and

the North, especially after the Somerset & Dorset line ceased to be used for through holiday trains.

In contrast to the photograph of the 'Lord Nelson', No 34105 is coming under the bridge that carries a country road towards Silchester, with a southbound summer Saturday working for Bournemouth.

Goring troughs: 'County' 4-6-0 No 1006 *County of Cornwall*, unidentified 'Castle' 4-6-0

Goring troughs was a 'must visit' location in steam days, especially on a summer Saturday when there was a constant procession of trains in each direction. Flanked by the impressive telegraph pole route on both sides of the line, the 'County' is taking water as it heads west with a train from Paddington.

In the opposite direction the troughs are highlighted by the afternoon sun as a 'Castle' speeds towards Reading on the up relief line, with a smart train mainly composed of BR Mark 1 stock.

Near Finstock: 'Castle' 4-6-0 No 7032 *Denbigh Castle*
I spent many happy hours photographing trains on the Oxford to Worcester line, and this was one of my favourite locations, south of Finstock in the valley of the River Evenlode, which can be seen at the bottom left of the picture. The 'Castle' is on a Worcester to Paddington working on 11 May 1963.

Above **Standish Junction: 'Jubilee' 4-6-0, '9400' 0-6-0PT**
Some 7 miles south-west of Gloucester is Standish Junction, where the Midland and Great Western lines diverge, having run parallel from the cathedral city. This stretch of line was sometimes the scene of 'races' between trains, such as in this picture where the 'Jubilee' is making every effort to overtake the much more lightly loaded pannier tank on a local train for the Stroud line.

Below **Gloucester Central: '5100' 2-6-2T, '1400' 0-4-2T No 1472, 'Hall' 4-6-0 No 6948 *Holbrooke Hall*, '4300' 2-6-0**
It is May 1957 and I am on my way home after 'demob' at RAF Innsworth, having completed my two years of National Service. Before catching the train back to Paddington I am able to capture this pleasing scene of four locomotives at the station. No 1472 will be waiting to leave with an auto-train working to Chalford.

Bristol Temple Meads: 'Castle' 4-6-0 No 7024 *Powis Castle*; '4500' 2-6-2T No 5530, 'Castle' 4-6-0 No 4081 *Warwick Castle*, unidentified 'Castle' 4-6-0

A friend and I have made a trip to Bristol on 'The Bristolian' behind 'Castle' No 7024 *Powis Castle* to experience the exhilarating high-speed running that could be enjoyed on this train, especially down Dauntsey bank, one of the final flowerings of Western Region steam. In 1958 the train left Paddington at 8.45am, running non-stop to Bristol where it was due at 10.30am. I have photographed the train just after it has arrived and there are one or two enthusiasts standing by the cab. They are quite likely to be congratulating the driver on a fine run, especially as the station clock in the background seems to be showing about 10.25.

Before returning to Paddington I took the other picture at the London end of the station, which captures something of the busy atmosphere of Temple Meads.

Llandevenny: '2251' 0-6-0, 'Castle' 4-6-0

At Llandevenny, close to Magor, between Newport and Severn Tunnel Junction, engineering work has closed the main line so the 'Castle', on an up express, has had to use the goods line to continue its journey east.

Above **King's Sutton: 'Castle' 4-6-0 No 4086 *Builth Castle***
One of the delights of the steam era was being able to photograph the succession of extra trains that could be seen on summer Saturdays. On 15 July 1961 the 8.47am (SO) Ramsgate to Wolverhampton train is passing King's Sutton Junction. On the right of the picture is the line from Kingham and Chipping Norton, a GWR lower-quadrant signal protecting the junction.

Below **Hungerford: '4700' 2-8-0 No 4708**
Because of the volume of extra trains at holiday times, the '4700' Class 2-8-0s were pressed into service on passenger duties with some success, such as this summer Saturday up express, the 8.20am Penzance to Paddington on 5 September 1959. The use of '4700s' on these workings set a precedent, because a little later on Standard '9F' 2-10-0s were used on passenger train duties involving some high-speed running for what was essentially a heavy freight locomotive.

Opposite page **Near Teignmouth: 'Hall' 4-6-0 No 4985** ***Allesley Hall***

Folkestone Warren: 'C' 0-6-0 No 31112
Although the locations depicted in these two pictures are the best part of 250 miles apart, both are set in spectacular stretches of our coast bordered by impressive cliffs. You can almost feel the fresh breeze coming off the sea on this lovely summer day in 1959 at Teignmouth as a family group watch the 'Hall' pass by on a westbound train.

By contrast the Warren was and still is a deserted and slightly mysterious place, the railway dwarfed by the towering chalk cliffs. Not long before electric services began, the 'C' is on an empty stock working to Folkestone in 1960. Photographs can still be taken from the concrete footbridge in the background, though the view has now been spoiled by intrusive modern security fencing.

Right **Sapperton Tunnel: 'Hall' No 5980 *Dingley Hall***
Mellow Cotswold stone forms the setting for this picture of the 'Hall' emerging from the 'long' (1 mile 104 yards) Sapperton Tunnel and about to enter the 352-yard 'short' tunnel with a train for Swindon. This picture is taken from the A419 road, which crosses the line at this point.

Below **Spittal Tunnel: '5700' 0-6-0PT No 8739**
In distant Pembrokeshire, some 250 miles from Paddington, the pannier tank is climbing the 1 in 110 gradient before plunging into the 242-yard-long tunnel with a train from Fishguard to Clarbeston Road. The fireman of the pannier tank is glancing back at me, perhaps surprised to see a photographer at this comparatively unfrequented location.

Birkenhead (Woodside): '4MT' 2-6-4T No 42441

Flanked by what I think is a Ford Prefect estate car, the Stanier tank is waiting to leave with a train for Helsby on this quiet, still and sunny afternoon.

Above **Between Helsby and Chester: two '5MT' 4-6-0s**
The low sun on this summer evening provides ideal lighting conditions for this picture of the two 'Class 5s'
passing Morley bridge on their way to Chester with an empty stock working.

Right **Manchester Central: '4MT' 2-6-4T No 42455, '5MT' 4-6-0 No 44804**
Over on the Liverpool line side of the station, the two locomotives are ready to work trains westwards. The huge 1885-built GNR Goods Warehouse was closed in 1963 but, as a Grade 2 listed building, was saved and now has a new life as a shopping and entertainment centre. It is a reminder of the investment by the GNR in the Liverpool and Manchester lines towards the end of the 19th century.

Bentham: '5MT' 4-6-0 No 45140
Daresbury: 'B1' 4-6-0 No 61089
I have travelled by train from Preston in January 1958 to take some pictures on the Carnforth to Hellifield line. The 'Class 5', which is just starting away from the station with a train for Leeds, shows evidence on its buffer beam of having travelled through some heavy snow storms.

The 'B1' is an unusual sight on the Warrington to Chester line and is heading a London Midland Region excursion (1D37), probably bound for Chester or, less likely, the North Wales Coast, given the time of year. Since No 61089 was shedded at Lincoln (40A) around the time I took this picture, it remains a mystery to me why it was working this train. The locomotive was withdrawn from Colwick shed in April 1966.

Right **Tay Bridge**
Hauled by a 'V2' 2-6-2, its smoke blown across the river by a stiff westerly wind, I am about to cross the 2-mile-long bridge over the Tay on a train from Dundee to Edinburgh in the summer of 1958. The remains of the piers of the old bridge point the way to the distant south shore and Wormit.

Below **Lochy Bridge, Fort William: '4MT' 2-6-0 No 76001**
One of the first batch of five locomotives allocated to the Scottish Region, No 76001 moved up from Motherwell in the summer of 1960 to be used on the West Highland line to Mallaig, turn and turn about with the usual 'K1' 2-6-0s. However, no further members of the class were sent north so the 'K1s' continued to be the standard motive power for the services on the line. The locomotive is crossing the River Lochy on 27 July 1961 with a train for Mallaig. This view is more difficult to take now as a new footbridge adjoins the railway bridge over the river.

Above **Diss: 'Britannia' 4-6-2 No 70005 *John Milton***
Geographically this picture is out of sequence here, but I have included it as a contrast to the one of No 70053 below. No 70005 was allocated new to Stratford shed in April 1951 to work speeded-up expresses on the Liverpool Street to Norwich line.

Typifying the excellent work the 'Britannias' did on these trains, No 70005 makes a magnificent sight storming through Diss with a service for Ipswich and London. The locomotive outlived No 70053 by three months, being withdrawn from Carlisle (Kingmoor) in July 1967.

Left **Carstairs: 'Britannia' 4-6-2 No 70053 *Moray Firth***
It is nearly 10.30pm on 3 September 1966 as Carlisle (Kingmoor) shed's rather run-down-looking 'Britannia' waits to head what I think are the Edinburgh coaches detached off the 8.25pm Carlisle to Perth train. Although the locomotive has lost its name and original smokebox numberplate, an effort has been made to smarten things up at the front end.

Right **King's Cross: 'A4' 4-6-2 No 60028 Walter K. Whigham**
July 1959 and the smartly turned-out 'A4' is getting ready to leave on 'The Elizabethan' non-stop train to Edinburgh Waverley, arguably the last high-speed prestige service in the country worked by steam. Notice the coal piled high in the tender and the well-polished front drawhook on the locomotive. The train left London at 9.30am and arrived in Edinburgh at 4.5pm.

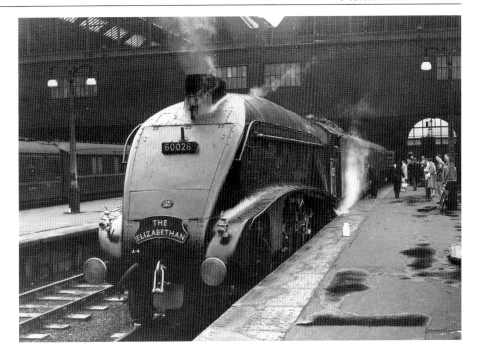

Below **Edinburgh Waverley**
Here is the destination of 'The Elizabethan', taken just before 5pm shortly after I arrived on the non-stop train from London. There is much of interest to study in this picture taken from the west end of the station, not least the lovely patterns of the track layout and the buses on the high North Bridge. The sombre bulk of the North British Hotel dominates the skyline on the left of the picture.

Left **Crianlarich (Upper): '5MT' 4-6-0 No 44908**
Overlooked by the impressive mountains that tower to the south-east over Glen Falloch, the 'Class 5' is coasting into the station with a freight bound for Fort William. The rather tired-looking station nameboard on the platform indicates that 'Refreshment Rooms' are available, a facility that can be enjoyed at the station to this day.

Below **Ardlui: '5MT' 4-6-0s Nos 44996 and 44957**
Regular motive power for the West Highland from Glasgow to Fort William was the LMS 'Class 5'. Two of these locomotives are passing at Ardlui – No 44996 waits to proceed south on a train for Glasgow while No 44957 runs into the station with a Fort William train.

Above **Georgemas Junction: '5MT' 4-6-0 No 44723**
It is difficult to believe that this remote and most northerly railway junction is 147 miles by rail from Inverness, even the fastest train taking the best part of 4 hours over the journey in steam days. The 6¾-mile branch on to Thurso can be seen behind the 'Class 5', which is pulling away from the station on its long journey south in the summer of 1959.

Below **Tain: '5MT' 4-6-0 No 45460**
103 miles down the line from Georgemas Junction, the 'Class 5' is departing with a train for Inverness.

Secondary and cross-country lines

What a wonderful collection of lines these were, but they sadly suffered badly under the Beeching Report closure proposals, leaving almost half the locations shown in this section without a train service. The West of England and Wales were particularly rich in secondary and cross-country lines, of which there are three that I especially miss. The first is the Somerset & Dorset (S&D) between Bath Green Park and Bournemouth West. At Bath the station happily survives as part of a Sainsbury's supermarket, but there is nothing left at Bournemouth, where a new road parallels the course of the line up towards Branksome. My first contact with the S&D was during a family holiday in 1953 to Sandbanks, now a very expensive suburb of Bournemouth. My father made sure we had a good start to the holiday for we travelled down to Bournemouth West on the 13-coach 'Bournemouth Belle' Pullman hauled by 'Merchant Navy' No 35018 *British India Line*. I still have my notebook that shows that '4F' No 44558 was at Bournemouth West, probably having worked an S&D line local train.

On Thursday 6 August I made my first long-anticipated visit to what was to me the mysterious and exotic S&D. I travelled from Bournemouth West on the 'Pines Express', consisting of 12 coaches with 'Class 5' No 44839 in charge. At Stalbridge I changed into a local train for Templecombe, hauled by '2P' No 40569, and on arrival visited the shed at 11.15am, where there were just five locomotives present.

Then it was off for a trip down the 'South Western' main line to Exeter and Exmouth Junction shed before returning by the same route, this time behind 'Class 5' No 44830 from Templecombe to Bournemouth West.

The second line is the much-lamented 'Southern' route from Exeter to Plymouth via Okehampton, which I first visited in 1954. Okehampton had the added attraction of being the starting point for trains over the charismatic North Cornwall line, some pictures of which are on pages 46 and 47. Although the track has been removed over the 20 miles or so between Meldon Viaduct to the west of Okehampton and Bere Alston, there is perhaps hope that the missing section of the line will be reinstated. If so, trains will once again be able to travel through the beautiful country to the north of Dartmoor on their way to Plymouth. But whatever the future holds, I like to remember the line as it appears on page 45 at Bere Alston, on that sunny summer day in 1958.

Lastly is the long line from Ruabon to Arthog and Barmouth, the most northerly of the three principal inland routes from east to west through the mountainous heart of Wales. Only a handful of trains a day ran the full length, taking between 2 and 3 hours to complete the journey, though there were a few extra workings on summer Saturdays. South-west of Llyn Tegid (Lake Bala), the railway ran along a lovely valley towards Dolgellau and the sea, with the mountains of the Cader Idris range in the far distance. This was a difficult line to photograph in steam days, given the sparse train service as well as the unpredictable Welsh weather, but I was able to secure a few pleasing pictures on the line including, the one at Llyn Tegid that appears on page 56. It is no wonder that the beauty of this line attracted preservationists both at Bala and further east at Llangollen, where 7 miles to Carrog have been saved. This is arguably one of the finest scenic rides on any preserved railway in the country. Another 3 miles on from Carrog to Corwen is due to be opened in the not too distant future.

Okehampton: '4300' 2-6-0 No 7335
To learn the two routes been Exeter and Plymouth, Southern and Western Region crews and their locomotives worked over these lines in case one was closed at any time. Here a very smartly turned out '4300' from Plymouth Laira shed is pulling away up the 1 in 77 gradient from Okehampton towards Meldon Junction.

Above **Between Edenbridge Town and Hurst Green: 'H' 0-4-4T No 31533**
The line from Oxted to Groombridge passes under the Redhill to Tonbridge line by means of the divided 319-yard-long Edenbridge Tunnel. Escorted into the tunnel by a helpful ganger, there was just enough light here for me to capture this unusual picture of the 'H' passing under the Tonbridge line with a local train from Tunbridge Wells West to Oxted.

Right **Groombridge: 'H' 0-4-4T**
As is obvious from the beautifully kept condition of the lawn and flower beds, the staff at the station have taken a great pride in their surroundings. This push-and-pull train is leaving for Oxted propelled by an 'H' Class locomotive. Although the buildings (but not the canopy) on the left of the picture survive, this scene has totally changed today and the line from Tunbridge Wells West to Eridge is now operated by the Spa Valley Railway.

Below Mayfield: 'M7' 0-4-4T No 30055, 'T9' 4-4-0 No 120
The ancient parish church of St Dunstan stands proud on the skyline on the perfect summer evening of 24 June 1962 as the two locomotives pull out of Mayfield on the 'Cuckoo line'. The nicely cleaned 'M7' assisted the 'T9' from Eastbourne to Rotherfield with the Locomotive Club of Great Britain's 'Sussex Coast Limited', whence the 4-4-0 took the train on to London Bridge. I later photographed the special again on Brambletye bank on the climb from Forest Row to East Grinstead. Just look at the immaculate condition of the embankment and track – what a tragedy all this was lost when the line closed completely in 1968.

Above **Somerhill Tunnel: '4MT' 2-6-4T No 80147**

No 80147 was one of the class built at Brighton in 1956, and replaced the older pre-Grouping designs on local trains in Kent and Sussex such as the 'L' Class depicted in the picture below. The Brighton-shedded locomotive has just passed through the 410-yard-long tunnel not long after leaving Tonbridge on a train to its home town via Tunbridge Wells West and Eridge.

Right **Tunbridge Wells Central: 'L' 4-4-0 No 31771**

Further down the line at Tunbridge Wells in the summer of 1958, Tonbridge shed's old 4-4-0 is pulling out of the station with a train for Brighton consisting of a grubby looking 'birdcage' set, which is just emerging from the gloom of the station. Nos 31768 and 31771 were the last of the class to survive, being scrapped in December 1961.

Above **Leaving Guildford: 'N' 2-6-0 No 31817**
I mentioned this picture on page 38 in my earlier Silver Link book *Memories are made of this* – on 24 December 1960 the 'N' is leaving Guildford on a heavy Christmas holiday through train from the South Coast to Oxford and the Midlands and is about to go under the A3 road. There is a climb of 2 miles or so at 1 in 100 on this stretch of line, which calls for some hard work. However, the locomotive looks on top of its job and, judging by its bright paintwork, has recently had a general overhaul.

Left **Shalford: '4MT' 2-6-0 No 76053**
No 76053 was one of a batch allocated to the Southern Region and went to Redhill when new in April 1955, where it often found use on heavy cross-country trains. Here it is on just such a duty. Having turned off the Portsmouth line at Shalford Junction, the driver of the 2-6-0 is opening it up in exhilarating style for the stiff eastbound climb towards Chilworth and Gomshall.

Above **Redhill: 'Schools' 4-4-0 No 30927 *Clifton***
I am standing with my friend Gerry Siviour on a mound adjacent to Redhill shed to photograph the 'Schools' leaving the station shortly after 3pm. It is on the through train from Birkenhead to Tonbridge and onward to the Kent coast. Just above the locomotive is the portal of Redhill Tunnel on the Quarry line from Victoria to Brighton, which goes under the Tonbridge line at this point.

Right **Nutfield: 'U1' 2-6-0 No 31903**
Some 2 miles out of Redhill No 31903 is coasting into the station on 28 January 1961 with a stopping train for Tonbridge composed of four Maunsell coaches. The 'U1s' were useful locomotives finding ready employment on the numerous summer Saturday holiday trains on the Victoria to Kent Coast lines in the 1950s. A few were tried on the North Cornwall line in the early 1960s, having been displaced by the Kent Coast electrification, but were not liked and soon returned east again.

Near Ashtead: '0415' 4-4-2T No 30582
On 19 March 1961 the Railway Enthusiasts Club at Farnborough ran this very enterprising 'LSWR Suburban' rail tour from Waterloo and back again via Staines, Windsor, Guildford and Leatherhead, not long before No 30582 was scrapped in July 1961. The day was blessed with fine weather and I have just caught the last of the evening light as the '0415' runs gently towards Epsom and thence to Waterloo.

Gomshall & Shere: '700' 0-6-0 No 30701
Betchworth: 'T9' 4-4-0 No 30338

On this cold day in February 1959 things must have been rather difficult on the motive power front. Very unusually a '700' Class locomotive, normally employed on freight duties, has been rostered for this Guildford to Redhill service. Its 5ft 1in wheels will have had to revolve at quite a rate to keep time on this service, which was allowed 10 minutes for the run of just under 5 miles down to Dorking Town.

Drummond 'T9s' were, however, more common on passenger turns on this line in the 1950s, like this very dirty looking No 30338, coasting into Betchworth with a train for Guildford and Reading composed of a 'birdcage' set. Other veteran locomotives finished their days on the Redhill to Reading line in the 1950s such as the 'D' and 'E' Class 4-4-0s.

Above **Stockbridge: 'T9' 4-4-0 30287**
The late winter afternoon sun is catching the side of the boiler of this nicely cleaned 'T9', which is leaving the station bound for Andover Junction on its 50-minute journey from Eastleigh along the delightful valley of the River Test. The then almost new BR Mark 1 coaches in carmine and cream are in complete contrast to the Victorian-era locomotive.

Left **Holmsley: 'M7' 0-4-4T No 30031**
Situated on the 'Castleman's Corkscrew' line, Holmsley was the first station after Brockenhurst. No 30031 is arriving at the up platform on the fine summer afternoon of 21 July 1962 with a train from Bournemouth West to Brockenhurst via Wimborne and Ringwood. The line closed to passenger traffic on 4 May 1964, though the station house lives on in a new role as the popular 'Holmsley Tea Rooms'.

Right **Longhope: '4300' 2-6-0 No 7335**
With 19 miles to go to its destination at Hereford, Gloucester shed's nicely cleaned 'Mogul' is arriving at the station one fine evening. I have been lucky enough to capture perfectly the token changeover between the fireman of No 7335 and the signalman.

Below **Bere Alston: '4300' 2-6-0 No 7335, 'O2' 0-4-4T No 30225**
On the same working as shown on page 36, but in the opposite direction, here is No 7335 again arriving at Bere Alston station in the summer of 1958 while the 'O2', on a connecting service to Callington, waits in the branch line platform.

Above **Okehampton: 'Battle of Britain' No 34080 *74 Squadron***
The 'Battle of Britain' is running into the station with a summer Saturday train from the North Cornwall line with through coaches for Waterloo, and will shortly continue on its journey to Exeter Central. On the right of the picture an 'N' Class 2-6-0 waits to leave for Plymouth.

Below **Near Ashwater: 'T9' 4-4-0 No 30715**
On a typical North Cornwall line passenger working consisting of a two-coach Maunsell set and three vans, the 'T9' has a lightweight train as it heads towards Okehampton in April 1960. No 30715 was among the last survivors of the class, being withdrawn in July 1961.

Above **Wadebridge: '0298' 2-4-0T No 30586, 'Battle of Britain' 4-6-2 No 34069 *Hawkinge***

I suppose for many railway enthusiasts and photographers, distant Wadebridge was a sort of Shangri-La, home of the fabled three surviving Beattie 'well tanks'. To make a pilgrimage to see them you could have travelled on the 'Atlantic Coast Express', and here it is arriving just after 5pm, a journey of 6 hours or so from Waterloo. No 30586, which mostly enjoyed a tranquil life at Wadebridge as station pilot rather than working the Wenford Bridge goods, is waiting to welcome the train.

Right **Wadebridge: '0298' 2-4-0T No 30586**

Over on the up side of the station looking towards Padstow, the nicely cleaned 'Well tank' is shunting some wagons next to the substantial pile of locomotive coal. What appears to be an SECR 'birdcage' coach is parked beyond the turntable, no doubt being used as a breakdown van.

Midford: '4F' 0-6-0 and '2P' 4-4-0
This is perhaps a slightly less familiar view of this Somerset & Dorset line location, which was very popular with photographers in steam days. The two locomotives are heading south with a summer Saturday train in 1959. Visible below the '2P' is the bridge carrying the Limpley Stoke to Camerton line under the S&D, which was of course the setting for the 1953 film *The Titfield Thunderbolt*. I almost expected to see a '14XX' 0-4-2T suddenly emerge from under the S&D hauling an ancient coach!

Right **Cole: '3F' 0-6-0 No 43682**
In the late 1950s, before the 'Westernisation' of the Somerset & Dorset line took place, its Midland Railway origins are evoked by this picture of a southbound local train entering the station hauled by the Johnson-designed locomotive. The scene is greatly enhanced by the delightful and ornate signal bracket at the end of the platform.

Below **Evercreech Junction: '2251' 0-6-0 No 3218**
This is perhaps a less common view of the station from the north end and gives a good idea of the facilities available, including the goods yard with its shed. On 3 April 1965 No 3218 is shunting some stock out of the siding between the up and down lines, where in summers past locomotives like the '2Ps' waited to pilot heavy northbound expresses on the climb to Masbury.

Near Masbury: '4F' 0-6-0 No 44417; '4F' 0-6-0 No 44424 and '5MT' 4-6-0

No 44417 was a regular performer on the Somerset & Dorset and here it is shortly after having passed Masbury summit with a smart northbound local train composed of three ex-LMS coaches. Note the tablet-catcher apparatus prominently in view on the tender by the bottom of the cab.

At the same location, but taken from Oakhill road bridge, the two locomotives are almost at the end of the long southbound climb of 8 miles or so from Radstock to Masbury summit with a heavy 12-coach train. For good reason this point was sometimes called 'Welcome Bridge', as loco crews knew that the end of the climb, with its 1 in 50 ruling gradient, was very near.

Bourne End: '6100' 2-6-2T No 6131
Ross-on-Wye: '5100' 2-6-2T No 5182
No 6131, one of a class built to work London outer suburban services, waits at the station with a train from High Wycombe to Maidenhead. The bay platform for the Marlow branch is on the extreme left of the picture.

The family resemblance of the locomotives in these two pictures is fairly clear, No 5182 being the country cousin of No 6131. The '5100' is running into Ross-on-Wye station in April 1959 with a train from Hereford to Gloucester.

Above **Bow Street: 'Manor' 4-6-0 No 7819** *Hinton Manor*
On a wonderfully clear morning the 'Manor' is leaving the station bound for Machynlleth hauling three maroon-liveried BR Mark I coaches. While the locomotive is bright and shiny, the cleaners do not seem to have had time to deal with the distinctly grubby tender – or perhaps this was a case where some unofficial cleaning by enthusiasts had taken place overnight and they had run out of time to finish the job!

Left **Harlech: '4300' 2-6-0 No 5369**
It is a fine summer evening, providing ideal light for me to photograph the Churchward 'Mogul' leaving the station with a train for Barmouth, some 11 miles further on. Standing proud on the cliffs behind the line is the castle built by King Edward I towards the end of the 13th century, which made a wonderful backdrop for railway photography at Harlech.

Above **Pwllheli: '2251' 0-6-0 No 2201**
In this pure 'Great Western' scene, the '2251' is waiting to leave the spacious terminus station with a train for Dovey Junction, 54 miles to the south. The journey will take about 2¾ hours with some 30 stops on the way.

Below **Near Penrhyndeudraeth: '4300' 2-6-0**
The stretch of line between Barmouth and Porthmadog abounds with attractive photographic locations, though unfortunately the train service was quite sparse in steam days. Typical of the opportunities on offer is this shot of a 'Mogul' on a train for Pwllheli pulling away from the little toll bridge that carried the road and rail over the Afon Dwyryd.

Left Llanwrtyd Wells: '8F' 2-8-0
No 48434
The '8F' has stopped at this small spa town in central Wales with a heavy summer Saturday train for Swansea (Victoria). The wet weather has made the rails greasy, causing the locomotive to slip badly as the driver tries to get the train on the move towards Llandovery. No 48434, which carries an 87F Llanelly shedplate, later came down in the world, finishing its days at Lostock Hall (10D), a predominately freight shed. It was among the earlier '8Fs' to be taken out of service, being withdrawn in December 1965.

Below Llandovery: '8F' 2-8-0 No 48444
In contrast to No 48434's train, this was surely one of the easiest duties for an '8F', which I made a special point of going to photograph. The bulk of No 48444 seems to dwarf the single coach forming the 4.10pm (Mondays to Thursdays only – 4.20pm on Fridays) school train to Llangadog, 5½ miles down the line to towards Llandilo. There was no corresponding working in the morning to Llandovery, so presumably the schoolchildren used a normal service train.

Above Oswestry: '2251' 0-6-0
At the one-time headquarters of the Cambrian Railways, there is much to look at in this picture of the station, showing a train arriving from the north. On the left are extensive carriage sidings, while in the station two trains are waiting to leave. The station is dominated by the old headquarters building, which happily was not demolished but refurbished for further non-railway use. Sadly for a town of its size, Oswestry now has no railway connection, the nearest large station being Gobowen, 3 miles away on the main line from Chester to Shrewsbury.

Below Near Llanymynech: '2MT' 2-6-0
In this pleasant Welsh borders scene the Ivatt 2-6-0 is hurrying north with a two-coach train from Welshpool to Oswestry.

Llyn Tegid (Lake Bala): 'Manor' 4-6-0 No 7811 *Dunley Manor*
This is one of my favourite pictures of the Barmouth to Ruabon line – on this glorious summer afternoon you can almost hear the sound of the wavelets as they break over the stony shore of the lake while a train for Ruabon passes by. In the winter service of 1961/62 only four trains (on weekdays only) ran over the full 54 miles between the two towns. Further up the line at Llangollen, seven passenger trains each way served the town during the day.

Right **Near Abertafol Halt: '3MT' 2-6-2T No 82031**

I was probably hoping to photograph a Collett 0-6-0 or Churchward 2-6-0 at this attractive location alongside the Dovey estuary to the south of Aberdovey. However, I have had to make do with this '3MT' 2-6-2T, a class that replaced the ex-GWR locomotive types on the line. The train, which is bound for Machynlleth, has just come through a small tunnel on the headland.

Below **Llanbrynmair: '4MT' 4-6-0s Nos 75060 and 75004**
Together with some friends, including Roger Merry-Price, I made a trip to the Cambrian line on 13 August 1966 to photograph the summer Saturday extra trains. After a brief slowing for the station, which can be seen in the background, the two 4-6-0s (No 75004 leading and fitted with a double chimney) are setting off up the 1 in 52 gradient towards Talerddig summit with the 10.55am (SO) Pwllheli to Birmingham (Snow Hill) train. By the time they reach Talerddig the locomotives will have been climbing for some 13 miles from just outside Machynlleth.

Talerddig: '4MT' 4-6-0 No 75055, '4MT' 2-6-0 No 76047 ('Cambrian Coast Express') on 13 August 1966. No 75055 in particular shows signs Emerging from the steep rocky cutting on the approach to Talerddig, the locomotives of what I think was unofficial cleaning by some enthusiasts, perhaps the 'MNA', have steam to spare with the 9.45am Aberystwyth to Paddington service (the Master Neverers Association.

Near Llandre: '4MT' 2-6-4T No 80132 On a beautiful summer morning I had earlier photographed a Collett 0-6-0 near this location on a train to Aberystwyth, and the result is on page 61 of my previous book

Memories are made of this. No 80132, on a similar train, is working hard up the 1 in 75 gradient near the same place. Note the picturesque old Cambrian Railways fixed distant signal on the far right of the picture.

Above **Barmouth: '4MT' 4-6-0 No 75005, '1400' 0-4-2Ts**
This is the busy scene at the station on a murky day in October 1958. The then quite new 4-6-0 was built at Swindon in May 1951, one of the first ten of the class that were allocated to the Western Region. No 75005 makes quite a contrast to the two tanks in the sidings by the station, awaiting their next duties on the Dolgellau auto-trains.

Below **Llanbedr & Pensarn: '2251' 0-6-0 No 2237**
The smartly turned-out 0-6-0 is on the up Pwllheli portion of the 'Cambrian Coast Express' to Paddington, also in October 1958. The up train was hardly an 'express' at this point, since it called at almost all stations on its 58-mile journey to Machynlleth, which took no less than 3 hours. Anticipating the parking of vintage vehicles by the line on present-day photographic charters, there is a smartly turned-out delivery lorry waiting outside the station. It looks as if it could have been recently painted in BR carmine and cream livery.

Right **Highbridge: '2MT' 2-6-2Ts Nos 41290 and 41291**
Prior to the closure of the S&D in March 1966, the Ivatt 2-6-2Ts replaced the Collett 0-6-0s and Midland '3Fs' on the Highbridge branch trains. At the spacious station No 41290 has just arrived with a train from Evercreech Junction – sister locomotive No 41291 waits to leave in the opposite direction from a line that, unusually, had a platform face on both sides.

Below **Crudgington: '2MT' 2-6-2T No 41201**
A mere six trains each way, on weekdays only, called at this lonely little Shropshire station. The Ivatt 2-6-2T is pausing with a train from Crewe to Wellington. The gentleman in the dark uniform is perhaps one of the station staff hoping to collect some loco coal in his bucket for the station fires.

Stamford: '2MT' 2-6-2T No 84008
Ketton & Collyweston: '2MT' 2-6-2T
No 84008
The 'BR Standard' version of the Ivatt 2-6-2T was used on the push-and-pull London Midland Region service between Stamford Town and Seaton (Rutland). A Type 2 diesel locomotive on a freight train is waiting in the station as the train leaves for Seaton. Compared to the antiquated push-and-pull trains operated by the Southern and Western Regions, this 1930s LMS-built train looks comparatively modern and businesslike.

On a train from Seaton, No 84008 leaves the picturesque and delightfully named Ketton & Collyweston station.

Above **Oakham: 'D16/3' 4-4-0 No 62597**
Set off by an attractive Midland Railway signal, the 'D16' makes a smoky departure from the station with a train from Peterborough to Leicester on 6 June 1959. The journey of some 53 miles through the rolling English shires would take the best part of 2 hours to complete.

Right **Wellingborough London Road: '2MT' 2-6-2T No 84005**
Working the useful service that linked the LNWR line at Northampton Castle with the Midland main line at Wellingborough Midland Road, No 84005 is leaving the picturesque London Road station towards the end of its 13-mile, 25-minute journey. The train will shortly branch off the line to Peterborough, taking the spur up to the Midland station. The Northampton to Peterborough line closed to passenger traffic on 4 May 1964.

Fordham: 'B1' 4-6-0 No 61264; 'D16/3' 4-4-0 No 62588
No 61264, one of two lucky 'B1s' that were saved from being scrapped, has worked on the main line in preservation, notably on the Fort William to Mallaig trains. Here the locomotive is entering the station with a fast train to Harwich. The right-hand signal on the gantry controls the junction with the branch to Mildenhall.

A little later on this fine summer evening, No 62588 pauses at the station with a train from Ely to Bury St Edmunds.

Chilcompton Tunnel: 'West Country' 4-6-2 No 34006 *Bude*, 'Battle of Britain' 4-6-2 No 34057 *Biggin Hill*
In glorious sunny weather on 5 March 1966 the Locomotive Club of Great Britain ran its 'Somerset & Dorset Rail Tour' to mark the closure of the line. I had earlier photographed the two 'Pacifics' at Winsor Hill Tunnel (see page 125 of my Silver Link book *Thanks for the Memory*), then moved on to Chilcompton Tunnel for the return run from Bath to Bournemouth. This was a superb location for southbound trains as the line curved out of the twin-bore tunnel on a rising gradient of 1 in 50. The two beautifully turned-out locomotives make a wonderful sight as they emerge from the tunnel, a fitting tribute to all the trains that had laboured over the Mendip Hills since this section of the line opened in 1874.

Betchworth: 'U' 2-6-0 No 31799
There were many attractive locations on the Redhill to Guildford line, especially where it made its way along the foot of the scarp slope of the North Downs. Towards the end of steam working on the line in the autumn of 1965, this train has not long left the station on its way towards Guildford and Reading.

Baynards: '2MT' 2-6-2T No 41294
Baynards station, built to serve the nearby Baynards Park, was tucked away among the network of small country lanes that abounded between Cranleigh and Rudgwick on the Guildford to Horsham line. The Ivatt tank is pulling out of the station bound for Horsham. Baynards was famous for its display of dahlias, which in the late summer and autumn filled the flowerbeds on both platforms. Although the station closed on 14 June 1965, the building was still there when I last visited the area, kept in beautiful condition by its owner.

Haven Street: 'O2' 0-4-4T No W28 *Ashey*
Haven Street station is now the headquarters of the Isle of Wight Steam Railway, which has done so much to recreate the unique atmosphere of the island's railways. One still autumn afternoon not long before closure of the line, the old Adams 'O2' is pulling away from the station with a train for Newport and Cowes.

Above **Near Micheldever: Rebuilt Bulleid 'Pacific'**
Towards the end of a day of photography on the Waterloo to Bournemouth line I often ended up on the minor road that followed the line south from Micheldever station. As the sun set in the west some lovely silhouettes could be taken of Waterloo-bound trains as they laboured up the gradient towards Roundwood.

Right **Near Chilworth: 'U' 2-6-0**
The sun is about to set as this Redhill to Guildford train nears Chilworth in the winter of 1965.

This page **Lostock Hall shed: '9F' 2-10-0**
Rose Grove shed: '5MT' 4-6-0
Rather than showing the whole locomotive or train, there were plenty of opportunities when visiting sheds to take interesting close-up pictures such as the grimy wheels of this workaday '9F' and the oily valve gear of a Standard Class 5. How far removed these pictures are from the sparklingly clean locomotives we see today.

Right **Near Springs Branch, Wigan: '5MT' 4-6-0**
A picture that evokes memories of the last days of steam in the North West – one cold winter afternoon, the 'Class 5' is slowly approaching the bridge that carries the Whelley loop line over the West Coast route south of Wigan.

Langstone Bridge, 'A1X' 0-6-0T

At the beginning of November 1963 my wife Alison and I visited the Havant to Hayling Island branch to photograph some of the last workings on the line. While I used black and white film, Alison used colour and one of her resulting pictures appears on page III of *Memories are made of this*. The sequence she took was so outstanding that I thought it justified inclusion of another of her colour photos, which shows a train heading for Hayling Island.

Above **Ely: 'D16/3' 4-4-0 No 62610**
At this busy Fenland junction, No 62610 is slowly entering the station past the long boarded crossing
with what I think is the 'North Country Continental' train for Harwich.

Right **Haverhill: 'J15' 0-6-0 No 65456**
On a hot summer day in 1958, before the
introduction of new diesel multiple units
transformed local services in East Anglia,
the 'J15' is approaching the station with a
train for Cambridge. I had earlier travelled
up to Cambridge from Liverpool Street
behind a very dirty 'K3' 2-6-0.

Branch lines

When introducing the previous section of pictures I mentioned the number of secondary lines that no longer had a train service. Branch lines fared little better, for virtually all the lines depicted in the following photographs are now closed or have no passenger service. The Southern and Western Regions were the worst hit, with classic branches like Lyme Regis and Kingsbridge losing their services. Most of the lines on the unique Isle of Wight system, which were very much branch-line in character, went as well, apart from the section of 'main line' from Ryde Pier Head to Shanklin. The splendid Isle of Wight Steam Railway at Haven Street does, however, still preserve the special character of the island's steam railway. For those who were lucky enough to experience them, who can forget trips across the breezy Solent to the island using the ferry service from Portsmouth Harbour station, perhaps on one of the paddle steamers such as the PS *Ryde*. This 1937-built vessel still exists in a derelict condition on the River Medina near Newport, but renewed efforts are currently being made to save her before it is too late. Once on the island there was much to photograph, such as old No 14 working out its days in spectacular style at Sandown, shown on page 73.

Far from the sunny Isle of Wight, this section finishes with pictures taken on the most northerly and westerly branch lines in the UK and Eire that remained worked by steam. The Mound to Dornoch branch, which closed in June 1960, featured in my last 'Memories' book, but on page 87 I have included another picture taken on the line,

this time at Embo. Something of the relaxed and easy-going nature of workings on this branch comes over in this picture. With many level crossing gates for the guard to open and close, timings on the line were generous.

I had first visited Ireland in 1957 on a memorable week-long trip with the Farnborough (Hants)-based Railway Enthusiasts Club, although we had to contend with some persistent wet weather. By 1962 there was little steam working left in the country, but the rural branches to Ballhagaderreen and Loughrea had yet to see diesel traction. I am eternally indebted to Alison for her tolerance in indulging my wish to take photographs on these two branches in September 1962, but I suppose I can claim that these are now of historic value. In Ballhagaderreen we stayed at The Railway Hotel in Station Road and I still have a sheet of notepaper from it printed in Victorian copperplate script, which proclaims the phone number simply as 'Phone: 30'. In those days the economy of Ireland had yet to develop to the extent we see today, so donkeys and carts were still a common sight in the country towns. Recent pictures posted on the internet sadly show that little now remains to remind us of the charming little branch line stations at Ballhagaderreen and Loughrea. Later, on our way south to Killarney, we stopped briefly at Valencia Harbour station, the most westerly in Europe, at the end of the long scenic 40-mile branch from Farranfore. Although the line had closed early in 1960, a station nameboard still stood on the derelict platform – I wish we could have carried it home, and wonder if it was saved!

Brent station
I have just arrived at Brent on the goods train from Kingsbridge on 8 September 1958. Due to an oversight on my part I had missed the early afternoon passenger train from Kingsbridge and the next one was not until nearly 6pm. However, the friendly guard on the goods working, hauled by a '4500' 2-6-2T, very kindly allowed me to ride in the brake-van up to Brent so I could continue my journey. The locomotive has just come off the train prior to doing some shunting.

Middle Stoke Halt: 'H' 0-4-4T No 31308
Something of the bleak and windswept nature of the North Kent marshes comes across in this autumn picture of the 'H' pulling away in vigorous fashion from the lonely halt with a train for Gravesend on 18 November 1961.

Above **Bexhill West: 'H' 0-4-4T No 31519**
No 31519 is standing by the spacious platform ready to leave with a train on the short run to Crowhurst, where it will connect with services on the Charing Cross to Hastings line. Note the brand-new 'Hastings' diesel unit berthed on the adjacent line – partial dieselisation of services on the Hastings line began in 1957, being fully implemented in 1958.

Left **Lydd Town: 'H' 0-4-4T No 31521**
Although this picture was taken some 53 years ago in 1956, the line has survived to serve the nuclear power station at Dungeness and in recent years has even seen a steam rail tour hauled by No 34067 on 4 November 2006. Against the background of Romney Marsh, the 'H' is propelling its two-coach train into the station bound for New Romney. In the other platform another 'H' is waiting to proceed to Appledore.

Sharnal Street: 'H' 0-4-4Ts Nos 31193 and 31263
The two locomotives make an alluring sight as they await the arrival of a Gravesend-bound train before proceeding towards Allhallows on 1 August 1960. Possibly the train has been strengthened to cater for day-trippers returning from Allhallows.

No 31263 is now at the Bluebell Railway where, at the time of writing, it is being overhauled. The locomotive's plain but smart BR lined black paintwork is in marked contrast to the ornate SECR livery it carries at the Bluebell as No 263.

Above **Christ's Hospital: 'E4' 0-6-2T No 32515**
It is 3 April 1961, a miserable wet day that sees the 'E4' coasting into the station with a train from Guildford to Horsham. It will shortly join the main mid-Sussex line for the short run up to Horsham. On page 61 I commented on a line with a platform on both sides – here is another example. In fact, the station contained a further 'double' platform on the mid-Sussex line part of the station.

Left **Baynards Tunnel: 'M7' 0-4-4T No 30110**
This 381-yard-long tunnel was further up the line between Rudgwick and Baynards stations. The 'M7' is bursting out of the northern end of the tunnel with a train for Guildford. The narrowness of the bore can be judged by the steam trapped between the first and second LB&SCR coaches of the train. The BBC filmed *The Railway Children* at Baynards in 1957 and I think the area immediately in front of me may have been used for the famous landslide sequence. This was immortalised in the later 1970 film shot on the Keighley & Worth Valley Railway starring Jenny Agutter, and again in the Carlton TV adaptation filmed on the Bluebell Railway in 2000.

Between Steyning and Henfield: 'H' 0-4-4T No 31530

This train is on its way from Brighton to Horsham and is crossing the River Adur. There were quite frequent trains on this line, the journey taking just over an hour. Motive power was provided by Horsham and Brighton sheds, which turned out 'E4', 'M7' and 'H' Class locomotives to work these services.

Above **Hayling Island: 'A1X' No 32677**
No selection of pictures of branch lines in the South of England would be complete without one of the Hayling Island branch. Here is No 32677 hauling two old LSWR coaches on the approach to Hayling Island station at the end of its short journey from Havant.

Below **Lymington Pier: 'M7' No 30105**
On this day of heavy rain, my friend Gerry Siviour and I travelled from Southampton to Lymington in the afternoon to try for some pictures on the branch in the hope that the weather might improve a little. However, there is no sign of any sun as No 30105 waits by the rain-soaked pier before leaving for Brockenhurst, while to the right is the ferry for Yarmouth. The hills of the Isle of Wight can be seen in the distance behind the ferry.

Sandown: 'O2' 0-4-4T No W14 *Fishbourne*

It is a summer Saturday in August 1965 and still the venerable 'O2s' soldier on in the Isle of Wight. Suffering treatment not really appropriate for a locomotive 75 years old, No W14 is being opened up in spectacular fashion as it accelerates through the station with a non-stop train for Shanklin. The young woman leaning out of the front coach must be enjoying the sound of the hard-working locomotive but risks getting smuts in her eyes!

North Weald: 'F5' 2-4-2T Nos 67200 and 67193
Epping: 'F5' No 67200
Here are two pictures of the Epping to Ongar branch taken in the summer of 1957 shortly before it was electrified in November of that year. Two trains passing make a pleasing sight in this rural green belt setting comparatively close to London. No 67193, on the train for Epping, is fitted with an ugly stovepipe chimney, which totally alters its appearance.

At Epping No 67200 stands in the up platform before returning to Ongar. What a dramatic contrast is was to alight from a modern Central Line train at Epping and step back in time on the steam-operated service to Ongar.

Little Kimble: '1400' 0-4-2T No 1455
Bourne End: '1400' 0-4-2T No 1445

About the same distance out from central London as the Epping to Ongar line, these two branches were worked by the ubiquitous '1400' tanks. Little Kimble was about halfway between Aylesbury and Princes Risborough, served by not only through trains to Marylebone but also by this push-and-pull service between the two towns. No 1455 is leaking very badly as it pulls away from the station with a train for Princes Risborough.

At Bourne End the no-nonsense-style GWR running-in board proclaims that this is the junction for Marlow, the starting point of this push-and-pull train. Some services, like this one, continued through to Maidenhead.

Marlow: '1400' 0-4-2T No 1445
No 1445 was a regular locomotive on the branch and here it is beautifully lit
on this crisp winter morning, not long after leaving the terminus.

Witney: '1400' 0-4-2T No 1437
30 August 1958 was a glorious summer day and I have travelled with some friends to photograph the Fairford branch. I was always pleased if I could incorporate a church in my pictures – here I have been spoiled! The 165-foot-high spire of St Mary's Church stands out against the skyline as No 1437 is pictured shortly after leaving the station with an afternoon train for Oxford.

Above **Kingham: '5100' 2-6-2T No 5182**
No 5182 is leaving one of the up-side platforms to begin the short run to Chipping Norton with the afternoon train on 24 June 1961. Towards the end of services on the line there were but two trains each way on weekdays only over the 4½ miles. To the right of the picture are the well-tended station gardens, more of which can be seen in the picture opposite.

Left **Windsor & Eton Central: '6100' 2-6-2T No 6157**
One of the 2-6-2Ts used for the outer London suburban services is waiting at the spacious station with a through train to Paddington. Windsor Castle can just be seen above the station canopy.

Above **Kingham: '2MT' 2-6-0 No 78001**
This locomotive was one of a batch of ten allocated to the Western Region when new at the end of 1952. By this time allocated to Worcester shed, it is standing in the up main line platform in between duties. Adjacent to the large GWR running-in board, three members of the station staff are hard at work tending the station gardens, which are also depicted on the previous page. The Kingham avoiding line crosses the main line by the bridge seen in the background.

Right **Woofferton Junction: '1400' 0-4-2T No 1445**
The train is arriving from Leominster with a train for Tenbury Wells on 8 April 1961. This push-and-pull service operated on a 'T' pattern, running between Leominster and Ludlow on the main line, with associated trips between Woofferton Junction and Tenbury Wells on the branch line to Bewdley.

Above **Stow-on-the-Wold: '5700' 0-6-0PT No 8743**
No 8743 is pulling away from the station in vigorous style, on the 24-mile run from Kingham to Cheltenham St James. The station, which was more than a mile down the hill from the town, was a far more modest affair than that at neighbouring Bourton-on-the-Water.

Below **Bourton-on-the Water: '4500' 2-6-2T No 5514**
On 30 July 1960 No 5514 has arrived at Bourton with a train from Cheltenham and is waiting to cross a train from Kingham. The small group of people further down the platform will probably be changing at Kingham to join a main-line train on the Worcester to Oxford line. At the time of writing the station building seen on the left-hand side of this picture still survives, but is likely to be demolished to make way for a new development.

Near Bromyard: '5700' 0-6-0PT No 4664
I am travelling on my Lambretta scooter and have just been soaked by a heavy shower of rain. However, the sun has come out in time for me to photograph this evening departure from Bromyard to Worcester Shrub Hill. After taking this picture and partially drying out, I remember I enjoyed dinner at the Hop Pole Hotel in the town, which included some superb roast duckling. Dinner would probably have cost about 12 shillings, quite a lot for me in those days.

Torpantau: '5700' 0-6-0PT Nos 9644 and 3706 I used a picture of the station on page 71 of my earlier book *Thanks for the Memory*, but such was the attraction of this location that I thought I would include a couple more here. No 9644 has just emerged from the 666-yard-long Torpantau Tunnel with a train from Brecon and is about to pass sister locomotive No 3706 on a train from Newport to Brecon.

Right **Near Torpantau Tunnel: '2251' 0-6-0 No 2236**

No 2236 is on the final stage of the long climb from Talyllyn Junction and is about to enter Torpantau Tunnel, but both ends were difficult to photograph as they were situated in steep rock cuttings. This view was, however, possible near the eastern end of the tunnel where the line was high above the valley, which contains streams running off the steep southern slopes of the Brecon Beacons.

Below **Pentir Rhiw: '2251' 0-6-0 No 2213**
Further down towards Brecon, where the line overlooks Talybont reservoir, the '2251' is arriving at the station with a train for Newport on this scorching hot day at Whitsun 1962.

Above **Near Mary Tavy & Blackdown Halt: '4500' 2-6-2T**
Not far from the Southern Region's Brentor station, I am in the valley between Tavistock and Lydford in April 1960 with my brother and Gerry Siviour, to photograph one of the infrequent trains on the Western Region route from Plymouth to Launceston. In the background is the Southern line from Plymouth to Exeter –

how exciting it would have been to be able to photograph trains passing on the adjacent tracks, but the chances of doing this were remote. Interestingly the locomotive has lost its smokebox numberplate and has its number on the buffer beam, GWR style. No 4549 was photographed like this in the West Country in the early 1960s, so this could be the same locomotive.

Left **Iron Bridge & Broseley: '4500' 2-6-2T No 5538**
My brother and I are on our way north on 22 July 1961 and have spent the night at Iron Bridge. We have crossed over the famous structure to photograph this morning departure for Shrewsbury, which left Bridgnorth just before 8am. By this time it looks as if the second (northbound) line through the station as been taken out of use.

Above **Churston: '1400' 0-4-2T No 1452, '5100' 2-6-2T No 5179, 'Hall' 4-6-0 No 4992 *Crosby Hall***
This is the animated scene at Churston on 3 September 1958. The '1400' is waiting to leave the bay platform for the 2-mile, 7-minute journey to Brixham. The main-line train is heading for Paignton, Torquay and Newton Abbot.

Below **Uppingham: '3P' 4-4-2T No 41975**
In June 1959 the old London Tilbury & Southend Railway-designed tank locomotive has run round its train. The faded-looking terminus station in the valley below the town was reputed not to have been painted since 1921. Note the LNWR vintage ground frame on the platform. Curiously a brake-van has been added to the usual one-coach train, which will shortly leave on its short journey back to Seaton (Rutland). No 41975 was withdrawn in November 1959 and the branch closed to passenger traffic the following year. The site once occupied by the station is now an industrial estate.

Above **Aberfeldy: '2P' 0-4-4T No 55218**
Like the picture of No 41975 on the previous page, here is another vintage tank locomotive at work on a country branch line, but this time in Scotland. No 55218 is getting ready to leave this small Perthshire town with a train for Ballinluig on the Highland main line from Inverness to Perth. The branch closed completely on 3 May 1965 and, anticipating the interesting selection of vehicles to be seen in the background, the site of the station is now a large car park.

Left **Connel Bridge: '2MT' 2-6-0 No 46468**
On 27 July 1961 Oban shed's well turned-out Ivatt 'Mogul' is coming slowly over Loch Etive on the cantilever bridge completed in 1903. This was a shared bridge between rail and road traffic, though vehicles were not allowed on the bridge at the same time as a train. Use of the bridge by road traffic to and from Ballachulish on the A828 saved an extremely long detour inland through Tyndrum. The AA Members Handbook for 1961 stated that the bridge was always open and that the charge for cars was 4 to 6 shillings, and motor cycles 1s 3d. The bridge is still open, but now for the exclusive use of road traffic since the Ballachulish branch closed in 1966.

Embo: '1600' 0-6-0PT No 1649

As I related on page 86 of my companion book *Memories are made of this*, the '1600' Class pannier tanks were sent to the far north of Scotland to replace the Highland Railway 0-4-4Ts that previously worked the branch from The Mound to Dornoch. In this unhurried tranquil scene, No 1649 has paused on its journey to The Mound,

giving the chance for a local to have a chat with the driver. The guard, who has just opened the level crossing gates, walks back along the platform watched by two interested onlookers. The leisurely pace of the train enabled me to take pictures not only here but at Skelbo as well.

Between Dunsandle and Attymon Junction, CIE: 'J15' 0-6-0 No 583
The Loughrea and Ballaghaderreen branches were the last two in Ireland worked by steam. Here is No 583 on a train from Loughrea to remote Attymon Junction on the line to Athenry and Galway. The day has started fine but the clouds are building up on the strong westerly wind blowing off Galway Bay. The Loughrea branch closed in 1975, but I believe there is now a private preservation centre at Dunsandle, the only intermediate station on the branch.

Above **Ballaghaderreen, CIE: 'G2' 2-4-0 No 654**
In September 1962 No 654 is being used on the branch from Kilfree Junction on the Dublin to Sligo line. These were reputed to be the last 2-4-0s working anywhere in the world, the final GER 'E4' 2-4-0, No 62785, having been withdrawn in December 1959.

The lovely little 'G2' has just arrived from the junction and is using the small turntable by the shed. A horse-drawn cart is ready to leave for the town with some items that have been unloaded from the train. The branch closed on 4 February 1963.

Right **Edmondstown, CIE: 'G2' 2-4-0 No 654**
There were two intermediate stations on the Ballaghaderreen branch, Edmondstown and Island Road, close by Loch Gara. No 654 is arriving at the lonely little station with a train from Kilfree Junction. The old wooden signal is quite extraordinary, though its function was a little unclear to me. The train did stop at the station but no one got on or off.

The locomotive shed

I suppose the one aspect of the steam age that is most difficult if not impossible to accurately recreate is the steam shed, given present-day health and safety requirements. A handful of genuine examples still exist, notably at Didcot and Carnforth. Being the base of the West Coast Railway Company (WCRC), which operates a number of regular steam workings, Carnforth continues to largely fulfil its original role. As shed code '10A', it remained open to the very end of steam in August 1968, hosting several locomotives that were destined to be preserved, notably 'Britannia' No 70013 *Oliver Cromwell*. Some parts of the shed at Carnforth are almost unchanged since its original closure to steam, so the open weekend arranged by the WCRC in July 2008 gave the public a chance to experience a little of the atmosphere of a shed in the steam era. Preserved too at Carnforth is the massive coaling tower; although not in use at the moment, it adds greatly to the authenticity and historic value of the site. I remember one still Sunday afternoon trying to find my way into Patricroft shed, Manchester – it gave away its location by the pall of smoke rising from the locomotives in the yard and by the coaling tower, which stood out like a beacon above the surrounding buildings.

I have tried to make the range of pictures in this section as varied and interesting as possible, particularly as towards the end of the steam era you never quite knew what surprises a shed would produce. Over the years locomotive allocations and duties often remained unchanged for a considerable time. However, as traffic patterns altered, perhaps due to economic circumstances or modernisation in the form of dieselisation or electrification, long-established shed residents would disappear for scrap or be replaced by less familiar classes. The rapid growth of rail tours from the late 1950s also brought unexpected locomotive types to sheds far from their own territory, of which the 'A4' at Bournemouth on page 3 is typical.

With the pace of withdrawals increasing, BR's main workshops could not cope with the requirements for cutting up, so sad lines of unwanted locomotives appeared, as I show on pages 102 and 103. For the photographer they were a morbid though fascinating subject, typified in the scene that met my brother and me when we arrived at Bo'ness dump in 1961. The extent of the dump was unexpected and in its way quite shocking, not only emphasising how quickly steam would disappear, but also recalling pictures I had seen of the rows of locomotives awaiting scrap at Swindon after the elimination of the Broad Gauge. Of course we had no idea then that an even larger collection of withdrawn locomotives would be established at Barry at the end of the 1960s, although happily most of these would remain intact long enough to be saved and live again in the preservation era.

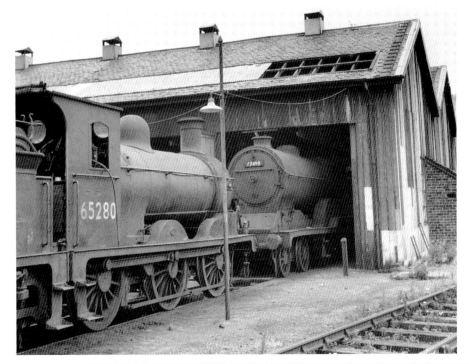

Polmont shed (64E): 'J36' 0-6-0 No 65280, 'D11' 4-4-0 No 62690 *The Lady of the Lake*
My brother and I called in at Polmont before going on to Bo'ness. The shed presented a rather melancholy sight with many out-of-use or stored locomotives – this pair were typical of what could be seen, the evocatively named 'D11' looking in particularly poor condition with a bent frame. Arguably the Scottish 'D11s' had the most memorable names of any locomotives working on BR in the last two decades of steam.

Weymouth shed (70G): '4MT' 4-6-0 No 75076, rebuilt 'West Country' No 34036 *Westward Ho!*

Two members of the shed staff contemplate the yard on this hot summer afternoon in 1966. Meanwhile the driver and fireman are preparing No 34036 for its run to Bournemouth and on to Waterloo.

Left **Feltham (70B): 'M7' 0-4-4T No 30042, 'S15' 4-6-0 No 30504**
On this cold winter day the 'M7' is running round the side of the shed near the coaling tower. Feltham's 'M7s' were employed on local freight duties and in the 1950s one could usually be seen shunting at the goods yard at Kingston; sometimes it was No 30038, which for a time was painted in Southern green livery.

Below **Nine Elms (70A): 'Q1' 0-6-0 No 33001, rebuilt 'Merchant Navy' 4-6-2 No 35021 *New Zealand Line***
By way of contrast, Bulleid power is on display by the turntable at Nine Elms close to the entrance to the shed from Brooklands Road.

Eastleigh (71A): '757' 0-6-2T No 30758 *Lord St Leven*, '700' 0-6-0 No 30695

Visits to Eastleigh shed always produced a sense of expectation as to what unusual locomotives might be seen, whether newly overhauled from the works or awaiting scrap on the sidings at the back of the shed. One of only two in the class, which were normally based at Plymouth Friary, No 30758 was withdrawn in December 1956, ending up at Eastleigh where it is seen awaiting scrapping at the back of the shed. Surprisingly it still retains its nameplates.

Less frequently photographed was the coal stage area adjacent to Campbell Road. The '700' is standing in front of two '82000' 2-6-2Ts, which replaced the older pre-Grouping designs on local freight duties in the area. Eastleigh locomotive works can just be seen behind the houses, in front of which an interesting selection of cars are parked.

Horsham shed (75D): 'E4' 0-6-2T No 32463

Quite apart from Horsham being my favourite locomotive shed (one of the few open roundhouses in the UK), this is one of my most satisfying shed photos. It has also been the subject of a splendid painting, which I have at home, by railway artist Matthew Cousins. The locomotive has just emerged from the shed to be turned ready for its next duty, probably a freight working. The worn paintwork has that wonderful oily patina so difficult to recreate on preserved locomotives nowadays.

Right **Bricklayers Arms (73B): 'Schools' 4-4-0 No 30904** *Lancing*
Not often photographed at this sprawling shed was the turntable situated outside the small locomotive works, which could deal with a useful range of repairs not requiring a visit to Ashford or Eastleigh. After servicing, the St Leonards shed 'Schools' will be running light engine to Cannon Street or Charing Cross to pick up its train. The turntable in the picture has survived, but is currently stored at Ropley on the Mid-Hants Railway.

Below **Camden (1B): 'Princess Royal' 4-6-2 No 46207** *Princess Arthur of Connaught*
Continuing on the turntable theme, the elegant 'Pacific' is being turned after working 'The Ulster Express', which originated at Heysham with a boat connection from Belfast Donegal Quay.

Above **Dover (74C): 'King Arthur' 4-6-0 No 30768 *Sir Balin***
Not only in the firing line during the Second World War, the shed was situated right by the sea wall and thus exposed to salt spray when gales blew up the English Channel. This must have made maintenance of locomotives more difficult than normal. Visitor *Sir*

Balin from Stewarts Lane shows signs of the care lavished on it at its home shed, where it was something of a celebrity locomotive in the late 1950s, though perhaps when I took this picture its heyday had just passed.

Left **Bricklayers Arms (73B): 'E3' 0-6-2T No 32458**
On a more mundane level, the old 'E3' is standing adjacent to the road that led from the depot entrance at Pages Walk to the main sheds at 'The Brick'. The steam crane on the left of the picture is of interest, and glimpsed on the extreme right is an SECR 'birdcage' coach demoted to departmental use.

Above **Norwich (32A): 'J15' 0-6-0 No 65471, Type 2 (Class 31) No D5574**
Ancient and modern side by side at Norwich in 1960. One of the shed's well-cared-for 'J15s', No 65471 built in 1913, makes an interesting contrast with the diesel, a type that was taking over so many of the passenger and freight duties in East Anglia at this time. The 'J15' looks well cared for and was regularly rostered to work the afternoon Ilford-bound milk train from North Elmham on the line from Wells-next-the-Sea to Wymondham.

Right **Stratford Works: 'B1' No 61003 *Gazelle*, unidentified 'N7' 0-6-2T**
I stand to be corrected, but I do not recall having seen many photographs of Stratford Works, which was integrated into the running shed complex. I took this picture on 14 March 1959, which must have been at a weekend, for there is nobody working on the locomotives that stand amongst the fascinating assortment of tools and components visible. The 'N7' is an auto-fitted example.

King's Cross (34A): 'A4' 4-6-2 60014 *Silver Link*, 'A2/3' 4-6-2 No 60519 *Honeyway*, 'A4' 4-6-2 No 60003 *Andrew K. McCosh*, 'A2/3' 4-6-2 No 60512 *Steady Aim*, unidentified 'A1' or 'A2' 4-6-2

Here is typical line-up of super-power at the 'Top Shed' on this rather murky day. Whether the locomotives were posed like this for the benefit of photographers I cannot remember, but the member of the shed staff standing beside No 60512 looks as if he is getting ready to tell me off, although I am sure this was a legitimate visit arranged by the RCTS!

Above **Willesden (1A): 'Jubilee' 4-6-0 No 45601 *British Guiana*, rebuilt 'Royal Scot' 4-6-0, No 46125 *3rd Carabinier***
Over at Willesden shed, London Midland Region motive power could not quite match the 'A list' locomotives found at 'Top Shed'. Nevertheless the 'Jubilee' and 'Royal Scot' awaiting their next turns of duty make quite an impressive sight, especially when photographed from this lower angle.

Below **Old Oak Common (81A): '4700' 2-8-0 No 4704**
A short walk from Willesden shed brought you to Old Oak Common, with its roundhouse layout, conducive to securing interestingly lit photographs. All is neat and tidy as the sun filters down through the roof of the shed to illuminate the '4700', which is possibly undergoing some routine maintenance. Of a class of only nine, No 4704 was withdrawn in May 1964, one of the last of the class in service.

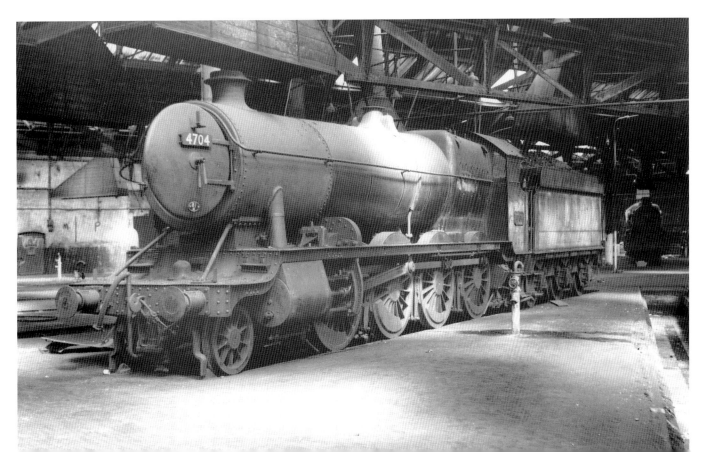

Above **Burton (17B): '2P' 4-4-0s Nos 40653 and 40655**
Especially as the age of steam drew to an end, you never knew what would be waiting among the lines of stored locomotives that would probably never steam again – a sad yet fascinating sight. Here are a couple of old '2Ps' that have almost certainly run their last. No 40653 is particularly interesting as it is fitted with a Dabeg feedwater heater. Both locomotives were withdrawn in November 1959.

Below **Burton (17B): '4F' 0-6-0s Nos 44434, 44599, 44436, 44475, '3F' 0-6-0T No 47643, '0F' 0-4-0T No 41536**
Inside the roundhouse, which has lost some of its roof covering, the six locomotives almost look as if they have been specially posed round the turntable. This picture makes an interesting comparison with photographs taken at the present-day 'preserved' Barrow Hill shed that regularly appear in the railway press.

Above **Camden (1B): Rebuilt 'Royal Scot' 4-6-0 No 46100**
Royal Scot*, Type 4 No D384, '8P' 4-6-2 No 71000 *Duke of
Gloucester
At the south end of the shed, the rebuilt 'Scot' is being shunted by
the diesel as No 71000 takes water prior to backing down to
Euston for its train.

Below **Saltley (21A): '3F' 0-6-0 No 43374**
In total contrast to the front-line-passenger-working status of
Camden, Saltley was predominantly a freight shed and in the mid-
1950s had a very large allocation of locomotives. I took this line-
up, which included four '3Fs' and an '8F', on the afternoon of
Sunday 24 July 1955, representing just a small section of the 112
locomotives on shed.

Above **Feltham (70B): 'D1' 4-4-0 No 31509**
As a result of the Kent Coast electrification scheme, several of the locomotives made redundant were transferred over to the Western Section, among them a number of 'D1' and 'E1' 4-4-0s. Excellent though they were, there was little work for them to do. Most were put into store like this sorry line of unwanted locomotives in the sidings by the shed on 30 August 1961. No 31509 did not last long, being withdrawn in May 1960 – all the 'D1s' and 'E1s' had gone by November 1961.

Below **Aviemore (60B): '3P' 4-4-0 No 54466**
Several hundreds of miles to the north, the scene at Feltham was re-enacted at Aviemore in the Highlands. This Pickersgill 4-4-0 and its sister locomotive behind are unlikely to work again and wear that portent of doom, the sack over the chimney. No 54466 was withdrawn in February 1962.

Above **Near Spalding: 'WD' 2-8-0 No 90286, 'O2' 2-8-0 No 63925, 'L1' 2-6-4T**
This little group of locomotives, which will have originated from March shed, is approaching Spalding across the Fens. The 'WD' is probably towing the other two locomotives for scrap at Doncaster.

Below **Bo'ness dump: '2F' 0-6-0 No 57366**
In the early 1960s the Scottish Region was withdrawing large numbers of locomotives as dieselisation gathered pace, and it established dumps of surplus motive power. Anticipating the famous collection of withdrawn locomotives that would later be seen at Barry scrapyard in South Wales, the dock area at Bo'ness near Edinburgh reveals a line stretching almost as far as the eye can see on 30 July 1961. No 57366 was formally withdrawn in November. Later on in 1961, as the effects of electrification and dieselisation become more pronounced, a greater number and variety of locomotives ended up discarded at Bo'ness.

Freight workings

Unless you had access to Working Timetables, photographing freight trains was generally a matter of being in the right place when one came along, so anything you secured was something of a bonus. The range of goods that freight trains carried was very wide, making for especially interesting pictures. A look through this section shows the carriage of stone, parcels, horses, cattle, sugar beet, china clay, milk, timber, general merchandise, coke and, not least, coal (usually for railway, power station or domestic use).

Frequent visits to a particular line often revealed the pattern of freight workings. An example of this was the early afternoon freight from Guildford yard to Feltham, invariably worked by an 'S15' or 'Q1'; pictures of this train appear on pages 108 and 109. Branch-line freight trains were of course more predictable and usually ran to a regular timetable. I suppose one of the most famous freight trains has to be the Wadebridge to Wenford Bridge working, which was in charge of the Beattie 'well tanks' for many years. My first acquaintance with the famous trio, Nos 30585-7, was during the course of my railway holiday to the West Country in August 1954 when I photographed No 30586 on its usual shunting duties at Wadebridge station. Four more years were to pass before I was able to travel to Wenford Bridge on the regular working from Wadebridge. This was possible thanks to the Southern Region, which, to its eternal credit, was very generous in allowing enthusiasts like myself the privilege of travelling on the brake-van of some freight trains. I still have the 'Form of Permit' issued by the Assistant Operating Superintendent at Waterloo on 29 August 1958 for me to travel on the 10.03am train from Wadebridge to Wenford Bridge and return on 5 September 1958, subject to payment of the appropriate fare. On arrival at Wadebridge on the appointed day I was issued with ordinary return ticket No 2654 covering travel from Wadebridge to Wenford Bridge via Boscarne, though I can't now decipher the fare charged, which is written on the ticket in ink. Both portions of the ticket have been carefully punched to indicate that the journey had been made! What a thrill it was to travel on this train with the friendly crew hauled by a nicely cleaned No 30585. The schedule was undemanding, allowing me to take plenty of photographs of the train during the stops for shunting, water and the lunch break at Wenford.

Another memorable brake-van ride with a train of stone from the quarries, was on the rarely photographed branch from Easton on the Isle of Portland, a picture of which appears on page 105. Looking at the detail in old photographs is endlessly fascinating, so I had always wondered what the Royal Navy vessel was that can be seen moored in the background of this picture. It appeared to carry the identification 'F142', so I assumed it was a frigate. However, a search on the internet revealed no RN frigate with this number, but my friend Roger Merry-Price suggested that it might be a destroyer, which indeed it turned out to be. Not long before writing this I was looking through a book of post-war pictures of Warrington at my parents-in-law's house. Turning the page, there to my astonishment was a picture of 'F142', HMS *Brocklesby*, in Latchford Locks near Warrington on the Manchester Ship Canal in May 1953! The ship is facing towards Manchester, so perhaps it was making a visit to the Lancashire city in connection with the Queen's Coronation.

Shipton: 'Modified Hall' 4-6-0 No 7911
Lady Margaret Hall
Regular visits to the Oxford to Worcester line in 1962/63 to photograph the 'Castles' on the passenger workings were always enlivened by the occasional freight train that came along. The 'Modified Hall', a class more usually seen on semi-fast passenger trains, is running gently through the attractive little station towards Oxford with a load of coal.

Above **Near Bitterne: 'Q' 0-6-0 No 30541**
On the industrial outskirts of Southampton the 'Q' is heading towards Fareham with a train of plank wagons. No 30541 looks as if it has recently been given a general overhaul in Eastleigh Works; it survived into preservation and is currently stored awaiting repair at the Bluebell Railway. It is now fitted with a single chimney, though I feel it looks more businesslike with the large-diameter version it is carrying in this picture.

Right **Near Portland: '5700' 0-6-0PT No 8799**
Not many photographs have been published of the branch to Easton on the Isle of Portland, but in May 1958 I arranged a trip on the line, one of the pictures of this appearing on page 58 of my companion book *Thanks for the Memory*. I am in the brake-van of the freight from Easton, which consists of three wagons loaded with blocks of Portland stone. With the naval dockyard in the background, the train is coming down the steep gradient on the east side of the island shortly before arriving at Portland. One of the vessels in view behind the cranes is 'Hunt' Class destroyer HMS *Brocklesby* (F142), which at this time was used for sonar equipment trials. She was commissioned in 1941 and paid off in 1963.

Above **St Denys: '4MT' 2-6-0 No 76069**
The tradition of lineside gardening plots is well illustrated in this picture of No 76069 crossing over onto the down slow line just south of St Denys station with a freight train for Southampton Docks. The locomotive spent its whole career on the Southern Region, being withdrawn right at the end of steam in June 1967. The locomotive was fitted with a BR1B tender with enhanced coal and water capacity.

Left **Shawford Junction signal box: '5MT' 4-6-0 No 73081**
The Standard 'Class 5' is heading north with a vans train past the box, which controls access to the Didcot, Newbury & Southampton (DN&S) line.

Above **Burghclere: '2251' 0-6-0 No 2240**
At this lonely station set amid chalk downland, No 2240 is arriving with a DN&S line pick-up goods bound for Newbury. Something of the extended loop installed during the Second World War can be seen in this picture. The two horseboxes next to the locomotive are a reminder of the importance of racehorse stabling and training in this area.

Right **Winchester Chesil: '700' 0-6-0 No 30316, '3MT' 2-6-2T No 82012**
Down at Winchester No 82012 is arriving with a DN&S line train for Newbury. Meanwhile the '700' blows off steam impatiently before proceeding south towards Shawford Junction and the main line with a goods train.

On Saturdays a favourite train to photograph was the early afternoon freight from Guildford to Feltham, worked by one of the latter shed's locomotives. The low winter sun illuminates the locomotive and the train perfectly as it heads north past a concrete permanent way hut on 18 January 1964.

Below **Between Bramley and Basingstoke: 'King Arthur' 4-6-0 No 30806** *Sir Galleron*
Displaced by the Kent Coast electrification scheme and sent to the Western Section, the one-time pride of Hither Green shed has come down in the world to work a pick-up goods from Reading to Basingstoke on 10 December 1960. When based at Hither Green, a predominantly freight depot, it was treated as the shed's 'pet' locomotive and kept in sparkling condition, with a regular duty on an evening commuter train from London.

Guildford: 'Q1' 0-6-0 No 33006

On 2 January 1965 the afternoon freight to Feltham is worked by a 'Q1' rather than the more usual 'S15'. Once again the low winter sun has set off the train to perfection, making this probably my best picture of a 'Q1'. A 2-BIL electric unit lurks in the shadows on the extreme right of the photograph.

Near Billingshurst: 'E4' 0-6-2T No 32469
More beautiful winter light, this time on the Mid-Sussex line. On 19 November 1960 I had earlier photographed the 'E4' on the Midhurst branch, but was able to catch it again en route to Horsham, after it had added more wagons at Billingshurst. The line is mostly climbing from Billingshurst to Christ's Hospital and thence to Horsham with gradients as steep as 1 in 100.

Wenford Bridge branch: '0298' 2-4-0T No 30585
Waiting by the line in this wonderful setting near Pencarrow Wood, all that could at first be heard was the rushing of the water in the River Camel below, then a hint of a soft chuffing sound and the squealing of wheel flanges on the rails as No 30585 appeared from round the corner, the wagons seemingly just missing the trees growing beside the line. Surely there were few other locations as special as this one for railway photography in the days of working steam.

Above **Tramway Junction, Gloucester: 'WD' 2-8-0 No 90710**
This was a very busy location where the Western Region and London Midland Region lines met. Consequently a wide range of locomotives could be seen, such as 'Castles' on Paddington services and 'Jubilees' on Bristol to Birmingham trains, with a myriad of other freight and local workings. Because of the number of trains, the gates on the level crossing by the signal box must have remained closed to road traffic for much of the time. The 'WD' is slowly coming towards Gloucester Central station past the Western Region shed (85B).

Below **Haddenham: '4MT' 4-6-0 No 75003, 'WD' 2-8-0 No 90630**
Apart from Ilmer Halt, Haddenham was the first proper station north of Princes Risborough. It had two through roads, which allowed the frequent expresses to and from Birmingham Snow Hill to pass stopping trains and freights. I have been lucky here to be in the right place to photograph these two freight trains passing, the 'WD' trundling slowly north with what looks like a rake of empty coal trucks. No 75003 was one of the class allocated to the Western Region, which later fitted it with a double chimney.

Above **Shepton Mallet (Charlton Road): '7F' 2-8-0 No 53802**
One of the charismatic Somerset & Dorset Railway 2-8-0s has just crossed the impressive curved 27-arch 317-yard-long Charlton Viaduct, which can be seen in the background. It is slowing approaching the station with a southbound freight that contains some loaded coal wagons from Radstock Colliery.

Right **Brimscombe: '9F' 2-10-0 No 92211**
Old Oak Common shed's '9F', on a partially fitted freight, is about to commence the steepest part of the climb towards Sapperton Tunnel. A banking locomotive was stabled here for use on up trains, but I am not sure whether the '9F' was going to stop for assistance.

Frampton Mansell: 'Hall' 4-6-0 No 4983 *Albert Hall*

Mist is hanging in the valley as the ex-works 'Hall' nears Sapperton Tunnel with a freight from Gloucester, banked in the rear by a 2-6-2T that will have come on at Brimscombe. The gradient on this section of the line is 1 in 60 at Frampton signal box.

Above **Clarbeston Road: 'Hall' 4-6-0**
The 'Hall' is slowly pulling away from the station with an eastbound freight train that includes two cattle wagons containing livestock, probably loaded at Fishguard. The superb condition of the permanent way is worthy of note, with barely a stone out of place, a tribute to the gangers who worked on this stretch of line.

Below **Sonning cutting: 'Castle' 4-6-0**
The 'Castle' is heading into the cutting with a train of empty six-wheeled milk tanks from West London destined for the West Country. There were corresponding workings on the Southern Region to and from destinations on the Salisbury to Exeter line.

Above **Woodford Halse: '4MT' 2-6-4T No 42250**
This train of empty coal wagons returning to the Midlands is signalled into the down loop platform at the station. A Fairburn tank locomotive was quite unusual on these trains, more frequently worked by '9F' 2-10-0s. The train is about to cross the junction with the former Stratford-upon-Avon & Midland Junction line, which comes in from the left. At the time of writing a Fairburn tank from the Lakeside Railway was visiting the Great Central Railway at Loughborough, so a representative of the class can once again be seen on the GC main line.

Below **Pleck Junction, Walsall: 'G2' 0-8-0 No 49328**
I have to thank John Edgington's detailed knowledge of the complex of lines in the West Midlands for identifying the exact location of this photograph. With three coke wagons behind the tender, the 'G2' is heading along the line to Dudley, while the line on the right goes off towards Bescot. Walsall football ground is located in the background behind the trees.

Above **Shugborough Tunnel: 'G2' 0-8-0 No 49126**
This double-track, rather than four-track, section of the West Coast Main Line between Colwich Junction and Milford & Brocton, is a bottleneck even today. The 0-8-0 will need to get a move on to avoid delaying up expresses to Euston, but with his locomotive clearly having a good head of steam, the fireman can at least afford to take things easy. The train has just emerged from the 777-yard-long Shugborough Tunnel, which takes the line under the Shugborough estate, the historic home of the Earls of Lichfield.

Right **Grange-over-Sands: '4F' 0-6-0 No 44399**
On 22 July 1961 the '4F' has just left this pleasant Lancashire resort and is about to pass Holme Island crossing with a freight for Carnforth.

Carnforth: '5MT' 4-6-0

The 'Class 5' is slowly pulling away from Carnforth and has just crossed the West Coast Main Line on its way to Wennington and Hellifield. On this fine summer evening the sun is low in the west, providing dramatic lighting conditions.

Above **Preston Brook: '5MT' 4-6-0 No 44692**
Not long after having left Warrington, No 44692 is heading south with a partially fitted freight. Out of sight behind the embankment on the right-hand side of the picture is the Bridgewater Canal.

Right **Stainforth: '5MT' 4-6-0 No 45204**
The fine dry stone wall sets off the 'Class 5', which has begun the long climb towards Blea Moor with a northbound partially fitted freight in September 1966. The position of the small overbridge in the far distance gives some idea of the steepness of the climb, the gradient being 1 in 100 at this point.

Above **Mildenhall: '2MT' 2-6-0 No 46469**
The branch to Mildenhall became quite famous among railway photographers and enthusiasts in the late 1950s as the last place where the Great Eastern-built 2-4-0 'E4' Class could be seen, notably the now preserved No 62785, which was withdrawn in December 1959. In contrast, the utilitarian though eminently useful 2-6-0 is waiting to leave the neatly kept terminus with the pick-up goods for Cambridge. To the left of the substantial signal box are some fine station gardens, almost worthy of a stately home.

Below **Near Whitemoor Yard: '4F' 0-6-0 No 44260**
The '4F', which has come from the Peterborough direction, has stopped by Twenty Foot Drain signal box and is about to back into the yard with a train of coal wagons. This was an incredibly busy spot even on a Saturday afternoon, when a constant procession of trains, hauled by a wide variety of motive power, could be seen working to and from the yard.

Near Scunthorpe & Frodingham: 'B1' 4-6-0 No 61021 *Reitbok* York shed's nicely cleaned 'B1' is coming up the steep gradient towards Scunthorpe from the valley of the River Trent at Althorpe with a loaded coal train. I had earlier photographed this train at Keadby lifting bridge where the line crosses the Trent and the result is shown on page 110 in *Memories are made of this.*

Above **Bedlington: 'Q6' 0-8-0**
Here is a typical everyday scene at Bedlington, between Ashington and Blyth. Local residents pass the time of day by the level crossing, indifferent to the 'Q6' rumbling by with a loaded coal train.

Below **Cambois: 'K1' 2-6-0 No 62011**
This picture, taken on 7 September 1966, conveys something of the atmosphere of this mining area – artisans' cottages, the level crossing with its ornate footbridge, the substantial signal box, a period road coach and, of course, the austere chapel, all set against the background of the North Sea. The 'K1' is heading towards Blyth with a loaded coal train from Ashington Colliery.

North Blyth: 'J27' 0-6-0 No 65860
No 65860 makes a pleasing sight leaving Blyth with a short train of empty coal wagons. Standing in front of the shed to the left of the train is a Gresley coach downgraded for motive power departmental use. In contrast to the rather drab industrial surroundings, an attempt has been made to smarten up the gravelled area at the front of the photograph.

Above **Roxburgh Junction: 'D34' 4-4-0 No 62484** *Glen Lyon*
On page 119 of my book *Thanks for the Memory*, I related how my brother and I tracked down one of the last working 'Glens' and photographed it near Maxton on 1 August 1961. Here is the same train just before it left Roxburgh Junction with the goods from Jedburgh. How well-tended the station flowerbeds are – I wonder if that delightful station seat and the 'Roxburgh' totems have survived.

Left **Near Kentallen: '3F' 0-6-0**
This picture shows a goods train on the branch bound for Connel Ferry on 28 July 1961. With its bent framing and lack of smokebox numberplate, the old Caledonian Railway locomotive has seen better days and it almost looks as if has come back from the dead – perhaps it is the nearest I will ever get to photographing a ghost train.

Right **Dysart: 'J37' 0-6-0 No 64618**
The last three pictures in this book were taken in September 1966 during a railway photographic trip I made with my friend Roger Merry-Price to Scotland and points south. The 'J37', in charge of loaded coal wagons from the colliery, seems to be ignoring the signal (which looks as if it is still in the 'on' position) and is about to cross a local road. The smart little car – a new Fiat 500, I think – waits patiently for the train to pass, but such is the modest height of the level crossing gates, it seems almost as if it could hop over them!

Below **Leslie: 'J38' 0-6-0 No 65901**
I am not sure what is going on here – the 'J38' looks as if it is about to cross the road where a Mini van is waiting to pass. However, the guard is by the gates on the other side of the line. Such is the position of the Mini that he could not close the other set. However, that said, I think it is a delightful little cameo showing a typical branch-line goods train towards the end of the steam era.

Burntisland: 'J38' 0-6-0
The locomotive makes a fine picture silhouetted against the waters of the Firth of Forth.
The outline of the Pentland Hills behind Edinburgh can be faintly seen to the right of the locomotive.

Index